W9-AFT-724

AMERICAN TRAJECTORIES

Warner Berthoff

AMERICAN

TRAJECTORIES

AUTHORS AND READINGS
1790–1970

The Pennsylvania State University Press
University Park, Pennsylvania

Library of Congress Cataloging-in-Publication Data

Berthoff, Warner.
    American trajectories : authors and readings, 1790–1970 / Warner
Berthoff.

        p.   cm.
    Includes index.
    ISBN 0-271-01051-7 (alk. paper)
    1. American literature—History and criticism.   2. United States
—Civilization.   I. Title.
PS121.B52   1994
810.9—dc20   92-41208
                                                                    CIP

Published by The Pennsylvania State University Press,
Barbara Building, Suite C, University Park, PA 16802-1003

It is the policy of The Pennsylvania State University Press to use acid-free paper for the
first printing of all clothbound books. Publications on uncoated stock satisfy the
minimum requirements of American National Standard for Information Sciences—
Permanence of Paper for Printed Library Materials, ANSI Z39.48–1984.

For Tirzah and Rod

Contents

PART III

Preface

The essays in this collection trace, in one fashion or another, the arc of emergence and ascent in the careers of several American authors and literary classics, and in the American literary record in general. Between the two speculative pieces that open and close the collection—the first on the historical distinctiveness of our literary culture, the other on the transition into the attitudes and imaginative preoccupations of our own volatile century—I offer in chronological sequence a set of individual case studies. The overall arrangement thus takes account of (and structurally matches) a pair of straightforward critical truths that nevertheless appear just now to deserve repeating and putting back into working relation: that (1) even in the broadest cultural and historical perspective, imaginative literature (like all the arts) is first of all a matter of individual signatures and differences, but that (2) there are also recognizable patterns and continuities that mark off what is distinctively American, what both reflects and speaks for a shared national experience.

The first of these truths—though both are of the kind one might reasonably "hold to be self-evident"—has gone oddly out of fashion in recent discussion. A bubbling ferment of new-New-Critical theorizing has latterly displayed aggressive impatience with the commonsense premise of authorial individuality and, correspondingly, with claims, overt or tacit, for the exceptionality of individual literary works and bodies of work. There remains, of course, a clear circumstantial reason why these once normative assumptions resist getting dislodged. Hypothetical negatives clinch the point. For literary making, as distinct from geographical or technological discovery and invention, if the publishing event in question had not materialized in one place at one historical moment, it would not inevitably have done so at another. If, for instance, the young Emerson had not succeeded in his private struggle to shake off debilities that by the time of his first book had killed off two of his equally literate brothers; if the New York merchant Allan Melvill had not reduced his patrician household to poverty and died an enfeebled bankrupt during the childhood of his impressionable second son; if Hemingway had been killed on the Austrian front in 1918 by the bullets and shell fragments that only hospitalized him for several months—or if, perhaps, he had not been wounded at all; or, conceivably, if Kate Chopin's enterprising husband had survived into a domestically agreeable old age instead of leaving her, abruptly, in her early thirties, a widow with six children, matters would have been—would now be—conspicuously different. And different, more or less, not only for North American literary history.

In any event, it seems demonstrably the case that accidents of personality and personal fortune do give a singular twist to what spins off the most overbearing *zeitgeist* or genre shift or shared ideological prepossession. The books we read, most of all the books we conspire to reread, come to us out of life-histories that are substantially distinguishable, and each such book, whatever its class resemblances and affiliations, will exhibit somewhere its distinctive lettering, its identifying signature. Such books can also, of course, be shown to have served in some measure the authority of one or another hegemonic interest; this has been the prevailing insistence of our current "new" historicism. Or else—in this new historicism's immediate precursor and mirror twin, the adversarial or provocation theory of literary production—they have worked to counteract or subvert some comparable ruling interest. (Are not the best books those contriving to do both things at once?—as *Don Quixote* famously attacked the whole estate of feudal illusion and at the same time affirmed a nobler, purer version of its self-conscious aspiration.) But they had in the first place to get themselves written, and it is with their getting written at all that the essays in this collection are centrally concerned.

The focus, then, of each of the pieces in the book's middle section is on a particular American author within the frame of a particular life and career. Or it is on some completed literary work in the discernible circumstance of the work's inception and execution. And though it has not been my over-all purpose to argue for the proximate truth of Scott Fitzgerald's assertion that American lives, for all the brilliance of their openings, do not move on to second acts, that does seem here to be a recurrent (though happily not universal) finding. If so, it is a finding that makes even shakier any tight linkage of individual literary accomplishment to inescapable cultural or ideological predetermination. The more honor, then, to the courage, the individual resourcefulness, or, as it may be, the sheer blundering opportunism, that has given us in the end so much that is genuinely worth returning to, and given it in such entertaining variety.

Concord, Massachusetts
November 1992

PART I

1

Continuity in Discontinuity

Literature in the American Situation

In one clearly documented respect the cultural as well as political and institutional history of the United States differs from that of other European and Atlantic nations: it comes down from originating covenants that lack— the Bible excepted—an immemorial authority. However privileged in common rhetoric, these covenants and written charters have remained vulnerable to the periodic recollection that they were enacted by identifiable persons with identifiable prejudices and life-interests who were responding to the predicaments of a particular historical moment. Accordingly, they may always be reopened, submitted again on any freshly contested issue of consequence to point-for-point renegotiation. So in national politics, although the 1787 Constitution and its framers are routinely glorified in public discourse, every actual or alleged historical crisis releases bluff new proposals for reinterpretation and revision, even at times for a new consti-

tutional convention to refashion a charter now suspected of being procedur-
ally inadequate and out of date. Appropriately, the documents themselves
contain substantial reminders of their own historical provisionality, as in
the counter-prophecy of possible failure underscoring Governor John Winthrop's "city on a hill" peroration in 1630 or the amendment clause—rightly
valued but all too often imprudently invoked—in the federal Constitution
itself.

By the same long-term reckoning—the native Indian patrimony having
been effectively destroyed—no North American prehistory intangibly con-
strains later choices and undertakings. For the dominant culture there is no
mystery of origins. A definite and memorable past certainly exists, but its
acts and assumptions remain at the mercy of present purposes; their intermittent sacralizing by interested parties and factions (or their demonizing,
as were in the Progressive Era the original Puritans) only confirms the
fitfulness, at best, of their continuing influence. There is indeed, we may
say, a historic continuity in American cultural life, but one of its key
principles appears to be a radical disrespect for cultural continuousness as a
source of strength and value, a measure of legitimation.

The American art critic Harold Rosenberg, himself an irreverent jack-of-
all-critical-trades, had a clear vision of this principled discontinuity, this
diachronic radicalism and fragmentation in cultural matters. The explosion
of "action painting" after 1945 crystallized his perception of it, so that
Rosenberg first tended to think of it as a distinctively modern (and "modernist") development. But the more he explored it as a determining attitude,
the more he had to acknowledge its extension backward across the whole of
American history. (It becomes, if we accept the analysis, one more exem-
plification of Tocqueville's theorem that the peculiar improvisations of
American behavior were a forecast of the general human future, whatever
offense they gave to settled tastes.) In anatomizing this "tradition of the
new," as he named it, Rosenberg understood that it was not simply an affair
of ignorance or forgetfulness, the uninstructed disregard of later times for
their forerunners' actual dilemmas and accomplishments. In America that
disregard repeatedly proved to have been part and parcel of the accomplishment itself. The "best examples" of American art, Rosenberg contended,
"consist of individual inventions which do not carry over into the future"—
in no small part because an indifference to the concept of inaugurating
transmittable legacies was as essential to their formation as an indifference
to receiving one and passing it forward.

As soon as we propose any such historical rule, important exceptions come promptly to mind. For American writing none looks more consequential than that of Walt Whitman, who offered himself and his book together as generative nourishment for the future and who in time became a recognizable—and recognized—progenitor ("pig-headed father," Ezra Pound would say) of voices as apparently different as Wallace Stevens and Henry Miller, T. S. Eliot and Allen Ginsberg. But the legacy Whitman assembled for his successors is, typically, shot through with self-denials. The poem of death that D. H. Lawrence saw all Whitman's work as composing includes, at its acquiescent center, the death, the self-immolation, of the poet's own life-project. "Who learns my lesson complete" learns first of all that "it is no lesson." Its best effect will be to open the field again (the metaphor of another neo-Whitmanian, the San Francisco poet Robert Duncan) and leave it clear for something equally self-engendered and, in turn, self-denying; in the end it only "lets down the bars to a good lesson, / And that to another, and every one to another still." Whitman's delivered achievement is thus, in his own eyes, not finally to be different from what, early on, he had said of Homer's and Virgil's, Shakespeare's and Tennyson's. To the ever-devouring present it, too, will in time be "gone, dissolv'd utterly like an exhalation . . . / Pass'd to its charnel vault." Even in its moment of triumph the poet's work is only illusorily an object to be acquired and transmitted for future profit, future Arnoldian acculturations (and Whitman, examining the Arnold of *Culture and Anarchy*, recognized at once a national enemy). The true locus of the work's value, for Whitman, is something that begins disappearing from it the moment it is printed and bound. The valedictory poem "So Long" sums the matter up: "Camerado, this is no book, / Who touches this touches a man."

For Whitman, as for Emerson before him, setting out to write his book not merely as if no one else had ever yet written to sufficient purpose but as if bookishness of any sort was a trap to the generative spirit may be seen as making a virtue of historical necessity. If he found in Emerson's essay "The Poet" an outline of what he himself meant to accomplish, he found little else in earlier American literature to help him substantiate it. More uncertainty hangs about Whitman's original project, the 1855 *Leaves of Grass*, than is commonly allowed. Even its grandly assertive preface (not, one discovers, a particularly accurate guide to the poetry that follows) has its hesitancies, its self-reservations. If the new master poet should find himself unready for his imperial task, "let him merge in the general run and wait his development." This, too, masks unstable assumptions. In order to have great poets, Whitman announced—in a proposition that became the magazine *Poetry*'s cover slogan during the literary renaissance of 1912 and after, though it seemed to the brashly contentious young Pound to have got the matter exactly backwards—you must first have a great audience. That is, you must be able to trust reentering that "general run," the common-wealth of everyday life and speech, to gain the powers you need.

For Emerson, however, it was just this kind of nourishing environment that America's "Jacobin manners" could not provide. "Why is there no genius in the Fine Arts in this country?" Emerson asked himself at the moment of completing his own first book, the apocalypse-minded *Nature* (1836), and gave as a main answer, "They are not called out by the genius of the people." Further, if some such popular genius could be shown to exist, would it in the end be any less harmful to self-fulfillment in others than either foreign or antique genius, with their distracting perspectives? "All genius [is] fatal to genius," Emerson coincidentally declared; "genius hurts us by its excessive influence, hurts the freedom and inborn faculty of the individual. . . ." The undecidability of the whole matter answered to Emerson's own ambivalence about native prospects, starting with his own. A deep-seated fear of inauthenticity, of falseness to some essential frame of self-being, seems the dominant motive. But this in turn, with its mandate to establish a wholly original relation to the universe, was undercut by complementary fears of solipsism and disconnection, above all of a debilitating private indigence.[1] There comes a point in one's march into life, Emerson acknowledged, when self-trust may become indistinguishable from self-deprivation. A single journal sentence in October 1836 anticipates failure even as it defines the extenuating circumstance. "The literary man in this country has no critic"; that is, no dialogic "other" to provoke him to his proper growth. The occasionally strident assertiveness with which in *Nature* and "The American Scholar" (1837) the still youthful Emerson proclaimed an end to America's imaginative dependency has this realistic assessment and prognosis as its dark opposite.

A conventional explanation for American-provincial anxiousness about inadequate preparation and the want of proper instruments and resources was the brevity of the country's "Civil History"—Emerson's phrase—and the unsettledness and unreadiness of new-world undertakings generally. Two

1. An emphasis anticipating Wallace Stevens's obsessive theme of imaginative "poverty" and also John Berryman's conclusion, under parental remonstrance, that he lacked "Inner Resources" (*The Dream Songs*, #14: "Life, friends, is boring . . ."). In *Emerson: The Roots of Prophecy* (1989) Evelyn Barish has given an authoritative account of the local and private sources of Emerson's performative uncertainties.

and a half centuries past the original English settlements the young Henry
James, setting off in the track of Balzac and George Eliot but conscious of
peculiar obstacles, could still decry "our great unendowed, unfurnished,
unentertained and unentertaining continent, where we all sit sniffing, as it
were, the very earth of our foundations." James's well-remembered list, in
his biography of Hawthorne, of all that was absent from American life and
culture, a list compiled by way of commemorating Hawthorne's struggle as a
narrative artist with the demon of provinciality, had been anticipated by
Hawthorne himself and by Fenimore Cooper as each described the special
difficulties besetting the vocation of authorship in the United States.
"Poverty of materials" was one such difficulty, Cooper wrote in *Notions of
the Americans* (1828). But at least equal to it was the absence of a distinctive
authorial tradition. (America, Cooper reminded his readers, is that country
which had printers before it had authors.) For Cooper the choice made a
half-century and century later by James and Pound, Gertrude Stein and
Eliot, and even, briefly, Robert Frost—to find a world elsewhere to do their
work in and have it intelligently received—would have been no more than
plain good sense. There is an abundance of everything "useful and respectable" in American life, Cooper witheringly remarked (himself in France at
the time), but the promiscuity of its development and dissemination will
indicate "but one direction to the man of genius."

2

Yet any such historical scenario, if we try to match it to actual events, will
be rife with contradictions. Cooper and Hawthorne are themselves conspicuous instances. At the moment of directing their energies to literature
neither was noticeably embarrassed by any lack of American materials and
resources; once seriously at work, neither wrote as if appealing primarily for
European acceptance. That historic accumulation of "picturesque and
gloomy wrong" that Hawthorne congratulated his native land on having so
far escaped, despite the inconvenience to its imaginative writers—this in a
preface (to *The Marble Faun*) written on the eve of a national war over the
reality of chattel slavery!—was in fact the substance of what his diligent
mining of colonial New England records and recollections had repeatedly
brought to light; its impingement on the lives of succeeding generations
became one of his richest themes. Also, the recurrent forms of Hawthorne's

storytelling patently borrow from and renew those of the black-browed Puritan forebears he apologized to for his frivolous vocation: the exemplifying moral fable or anecdote, the canvass of spiritual and imaginative "evidences," the expository divination of the "types" of human destiny. Cooper too, becoming historian and mythographer of two centuries of North American settlement and expansion, was following in the path not only of Walter Scott's Waverley project but of the chief secular enterprise of American prose in the colonial period: the historiographic chronicling in one new colony after another of new-world community building.

The guild industry of American literary scholarship has, to be sure, a professional stake in demonstrating recurrence and self-propagation in all sectors of the American literary record (a demonstration easier to bring off when the whole grand subject is treated in course-syllabus isolation). An inquiry probing beneath completed texts to search out their full historical origins—where, repeatedly, some European impetus turns up as decisive to renewal—is likely to suggest a different emphasis. (In outlook and practice the major American writers have been, in the main, less parochial than their scholarly guardians.) Yet across palpable gaps and separations in the actual lines of descent, similarities and recurrences do catch our notice; and if in particular we ask what it is that the writers in question have persistently chosen to write *about*, it proves easy enough to show that from the start American literature has held with remarkable tenacity to a concentrated set of imaginative subjects and themes.

"Theme alone can steady us down," Frost remarked (standing firm against the modernist dream of a wholly self-determined art). If we accept this as belonging to any reasonable methodology for literary historians as well, we find that a very substantial portion of the American writing that survives with imaginative force has attached itself to one—at its strongest to both— of two encompassing themes: (1) the covenants of settlement and community, projected but then in some fashion betrayed and broken in the vicissitudes of new-world history, and (2) the fortunes of liberated and unsponsored selfhood, male and female, within a social or else cosmic order that appears to punish success and failure alike with devastating impartiality. We may understand the persistence of these themes as a residue of older religious and sectarian passions. Or we may take them as embodying the anxious self-absorption of a massively triumphant yet contagiously fearful entrepreneurial majority. (Both views, in the Protestant-capitalist American context, carry conviction.) Either way, they seem deeply appropriate for a national population which has never yet achieved a steady-state communal identity; a people whose ordinary conduct required Tocqueville, at precisely the onset of America's self-transformation from classical republic to modern imperium, to float the Saint-Simonian term "individualism" in order to define what seemed to him a wholly new pattern of established human behavior.

Limiting examples to the period following independence and the first long surge of the population westward, we can identify a full-scale myth of settlement and its disheartening aftermath not only in Cooper's romances of the 1820s, *The Pioneers* and *The Prairie*, but, during the next decade, in James Hall's *Legends of the West*, William Gilmore Simms's proto-Faulknerian frontier romance *Guy Rivers*, Cooper's Templeton (Cooperstown) sequel *Home As Found*, and Caroline Kirkland's sprightly and self-mocking *A New Home—Who'll Follow?*; in popular works like *Mysteries of the Backwoods* (1846) and *Roughing It* (1871), but also, as a formative metaphor and counter-theme, in *Walden* and in Whitman's prophetic verse; and, taken up again though without discernible back-reference, in Willa Cather's Nebraska chronicles (*O Pioneers!*, *My Ántonia*), Faulkner's Yoknapatawpha saga (most notably *Absalom, Absalom!* and *Go Down Moses*), and, framing the separate "tales and persons," in *Winesburg, Ohio* and *Spoon River Anthology*.

But with each of these chronicles of settlement, the theme of selfhood— its prospects, actions, and ultimate vexation—at some point becomes equally compelling. The best, the classic American books almost invariably combine these dominant themes, as with the figural extravagance of *The Great Gatsby*'s closing paragraphs or, awkwardly and incompletely, the master-projects of Hart Crane (*The Bridge*) and William Carlos Williams (*Paterson*), which project both a personal and a collective myth. A casually brilliant early instance is Washington Irving's "Rip Van Winkle," refashioned from a German original into the first secular fable of, at once, lighting out for the territory (in flight from both American domesticity and, as it turns out, major American history) and reemerging an immigrant and stranger in the place of one's birth. A decade before, in the confessional romance of *Arthur Mervyn* (1799–1800), Charles Brockden Brown singlehandedly projected, though without American successors, a comparable double myth of, literally, diseased community and enforced estrangement and isolation. Titles tell us, normally, where the main emphasis is to fall, and the mode of narration normally confirms this emphasis. In Anderson's *Winesburg* an anonymous author-recorder overhears a whole community, one broken before it has properly formed, rehearsing its back-street transformations, its catastrophic secret history; in *The Great Gatsby* a specified first-person witness reconstructs the dream and its consequence, both grotesque, of a spectral alter ego and in the process enters upon his own unappealable American fortune.

When attention shifts to matters of form, and of expressive range, tonality, and purpose, the American bias toward first-person utterance can appear so insistent as to establish a kind of defining cultural voiceprint. The expressive seductions of this formal mode, in or out of the vernacular, seem irresistible. Even novelists of objective social interchange like James and Dreiser, Edith Wharton, Dos Passos and Faulkner, Flannery O'Connor and Norman Mailer can come through to us as extruders of visionary monologues. (Over time, Tocqueville argued, America's democratic-egalitarian society "turns imagination away from all that is external to man"; its subjectivizing poets "render passions and ideas rather than persons and acts.") In both prose fiction and poetry the collective first-person openings of the Declaration of Independence and the federal Constitution—"we hold these truths," "we the people"—break up into an infinitude of private impersonation. The work of coercing assent begins with an act of self-projection. "Call me Ishmael," "Let me call myself, for the present, William Wilson," "I celebrate myself," "I saw the best minds of my generation," "I am alive—I guess—," "I am a rather elderly man," "Here I am, an old man . . . ," "In my younger and more vulnerable years," "You don't know about me without you have read . . . ," "If you really want to hear about it, the first thing you'll probably want to know is where I was born, and what my lousy childhood was like," "I am an invisible man," "I am living at the Villa Borghese," "It's my lunch hour, so I go / For a walk," "What made me take this trip to Africa?", "In a sense, I am Jacob Horner"—it is in some such fashion, rather than with "It is a truth universally acknowledged" or "The Brangwens had lived for generations on the Marsh Farm," that the American literary imagination settles itself, in one text after another, to its chosen tasks.[2]

But for a full historical accounting the question must be: what imaginative gain is there in these recurrences and habituations? Does the earlier work effectively prepare the way for the later? Does it make easier or more incisive the discoveries and performative realizations that keep both art and con-

---

2. The phrases quoted will be recognized as the narrative openings of *Moby Dick*, Poe's "William Wilson," "Song of Myself," "Howl," a poem of Emily Dickinson's, "Bartleby the Scrivener," "Gerontion," *The Great Gatsby*, *Huckleberry Finn*, *The Catcher in the Rye*, *Invisible Man*, *Tropic of Cancer*, a poem of Frank O'Hara's, Bellow's *Henderson the Rain King*, John Barth's *The End of the Road*, Jane Austen's *Pride and Prejudice*, and Lawrence's *The Rainbow*.

sciousness alive? Does it help secure for them more appreciative audiences? Or must the game be started up again each time, as if only dead reckoning and the dismissal of registered landmarks will bring the writer through to where—"just go[ing] on your nerve," in Frank O'Hara's jaunty formulation—he or she proposes to go? An old joke from the complementary disarray of local American topography speaks resignedly to these analytic issues. Somewhere in the unmarked interior—Maine woods, Tennessee knobs and hollows, Minnesota lakes; it doesn't matter where precisely—a traveler asks directions to the next point of interest; after sober reflection the reply comes, without surprise: "Nope, can't get there from here." To "get" from one salient achievement in American writing to another can be harder than it looks. By contrast, French literature from Montaigne forward, or Russian after Pushkin, has both the appearance and the creative advantage of an unbroken household argument. Arguably the very continuities our scholarship has made more or less canonical on the basis, in succession, of Hawthorne's Puritan researches, James's critical reconsideration of Hawthorne's provinciality, and Eliot's insistence on "the Hawthorne aspect" of James's storytelling have muddled rather than clarified the business, with each of these authors, of accurate definition and assessment.

In any case the task of linking Roger Williams to Benjamin Franklin (both New Englanders), Franklin to Brockden Brown (both Philadelphians), the New Yorker Irving to either Melville (for travel description) or Mark Twain (for humor), Emily Dickinson to any male or female successor, or Cooper to Fitzgerald to Thomas Pynchon (see the later essay on Fitzgerald and Hemingway) is unlikely to yield to merely tabulative—or typological—explanations. Oliver Wendell Holmes, writing Emerson's life in 1884, postulated a direct route from Jonathan Edwards's reconstituted Calvinism in the eighteenth century to Emersonian transcendentalism in the nineteenth, a thesis emphatically enlarged and reinforced by the historian Perry Miller in the 1930s. Given the peculiar durability of the New England character and outlook, this historiographic route would seem a relatively easy one to mark and keep open; yet in the last two or three decades revisionist erosions and new-New-Critical frost heaves have pretty well shut it down to ordinary literary-historical traffic. Dr. Holmes also identified in Emerson's practice of poetry a technical principle—setting each line to "the normal respiratory measure"—which would resurface a century later in William Carlos Williams's open metric and Charles Olson's "projective verse"; typically, however, there is no evidence that either Williams or

Olson, at the point of innovation, actually considered the Emersonian precedent or even recognized, after the fact, their kinship with it.

3

Repetition without acknowledgment, renewal with neither the advantages nor the satisfactions of hereditary fulfillment—the pattern asserts itself so strongly that, beyond material obstacles, what we might also look for throughout American literary history is some active principle of deterrence, some peremptory inward resistance to any accreditation seen as deriving from past authority or proposed as essential to present and future cultural health. A sense of some such principled resistance and refusal, more dangerous to the commonwealth than mere ignorance of rules, fired Henry James's reaction, in 1865, to the revolutionizing poetics of Walt Whitman. (The really damaging consideration, James wrote, is that Mr. Whitman's verse does what it does "*on theory*, willfully, consciously, arrogantly.") James himself long afterward spoke of his brisk review of *Drum Taps* as a "little atrocity perpetrated . . . in the gross impudence of youth," but there is both force and logic in the argument it advances of a necessary sublimation of selfhood and merely personal striving in any art not self-condemned to eccentricity. The same argument, restyled into a quasi-scientific flintiness worthy of Poe, would organize the young Eliot's influential account half a century later of the necessary relations between "tradition" and "individual talent." It is a recognizably American argument, or counter-argument (oddly renewed, in an inside-out way, by recent American-academic speculations about anxieties of influence and a wholly burdensome literary past). The disposition it attacks is presumed to be both deep-rooted and long-lived, an aboriginal if not necessarily unremovable obstruction.

As indeed proves to be the historical case. The first *gran rifiuto* in American letters occurred several years in advance of the settlement of New England; it was the decision by the Reverend Mr. John Cotton of Emmanuel College, Cambridge, not to continue preaching in the erudite and "oratorious" manner that, according to his first biographer, had made him locally famous as "another Zenophon, or Musa Attica." Cotton's spirit "now savoring of the cross of Christ more than of humane literature" (John Norton, *Abel Being Dead Yet Speaketh*), he rejected an established virtuosity with school rhetoric in favor of the unmediated word and wisdom of God, to the openly expressed disgust of the university wits who had gathered to hear him. It would be stretching the point to say that Cotton's stylistic self-reversal founded a distinctive new-world literary culture, or that it histori-cally determined a similar confrontation in the other Cambridge two and a quarter centuries later between Emerson and certain scandalized auditors of his "Address" at the Harvard Divinity School. Nevertheless, the principle it answered to, a principle splitting open the religious and political culture of the Bay Colony itself within the first decade of its founding (in the Ann Hutchinson case), fostered at least two further centuries of invigorating doctrinal conflict and broke open that original cultural consensus into, so far, an endless sequence of contentiously programmatic reconstructions.

The doctrinal name this principle bore in the Puritan 1630s—antinomi-anism—is awkward to recover, though it retains real diagnostic value. But it was still alive as a fighting term during Emerson's nineteenth-century coming of age, to identify a generalized rejection of traditional forms and received lessons that could prove as cramping or narrowing as it was initially exhilarating. ("Beware of Antinomianism," Emerson told himself, as if to acknowledge his own fresh incubation of the old virus.) The unity even in dispute of the original New England culture is, of course, long vanished, and the active "dissidence of dissent" that, not less than the hope of a perfected covenant, fortified Puritan morale now finds expression, where it survives, in sharply altered contexts; but its latter-day dispersion and institutional centerlessness have not seriously weakened its attraction as a pragmatic alternative. To miss the antinomian solution's continuing appeal as a way of addressing modern discontents—paradoxically it works now to produce new secular orthodoxies, like biological Creationism, a supply-side political economy, literary-critical "deconstruction," or the New Pragmatist program, and passion, for purging philosophic discourse of "Philosophy"—is to find oneself unprepared for that recurrent moment in American writing, and in American behavior generally, when the slate is scrubbed clean, established practices and restraints go out the window, and a self-born purity of both intention and execution becomes the intoxicating new goal.

It may seem evasively scholastic to attach a seventeenth-century religious term and concept to the description of nineteenth- and twentieth-century cultural patterns. Yet to a degree that may call to mind Islamic attitudes and habituations more than those of the industrialized sister societies of Western Europe, American religiousness has tenaciously resisted marginalization in the power and legitimation struggles of modern mass society. The habit of dissidence, the chronic *ressentiment*, that are a main legacy of post-Puritan sectarianism have on the whole gained force within the national culture from their convergence with modern sociopolitical displacements and uprootings. In the contexts of secular life, however, this habit of disrespect for continuity-asserting authority, or for anything too fulsomely identified as established and respect-worthy, is probably better described under the secular heading of *populism*. But it is a populism, in its American manifestations, bent less on defending and restoring social usages overborne in the power conspiracies of modern history than on willing its own self-organized, self-determined, untrammeled, and limitless future. (There is such a thing, in the famously socialism-resistant United States, as libertarian-capitalist populism, and no one has recently proved more adroit at turning its ahistorical mythology to political advantage, consolidating the long national retreat from the ideal of a truly cooperative commonwealth, than the presidential regime it swept into office in 1980.)

What American antinomianism and American populism have in common as cultural universals is the dream of an exemption from history, an escape from either continuity or consequence in the cycles of elected experience. This is the real latter-day American dream. The original myth of a new historical beginning—more than that, of a new beginning that would prove the last prefiguration of the great ending promised in Scripture itself—persists, reduced and simplified, in the fantasy of a release from servitude to everything circumstantial and accruent in actual life. The society that, according to subjective need, would make itself over at every moment knows this servitude as its greatest fear; a servitude, or simply answerability, to the mere succession of what happens which (as Charles Ives acutely observed of Hawthorne's relentless narratives), though it is first apprehended as "something personal," turns " 'national' suddenly at twilight, and universal suddenly at midnight" (*Essays Before a Sonata*). It thus takes hold as the American imagination's defining nightmare. Exemption from history, and the retribution that the claim to such exemption inevitably enacts: isn't this the core theme and controlling narrative logic in such books as *Huckleberry Finn* and *The Great Gatsby*, *Tropic of Cancer* and *The Wild Palms*, *Catch-22* and even *Invisible Man*, books that in each instance were like no other in their first audience's immediate experience of them but for just that reason now seem to us all the more classically "American" in structure and motive?[3]

---

3. Isn't this also the imaginative condition argued out in that notably American (and currently undervalued) poem, *Four Quartets*? The mind-set in question here is one endorsed, if not anchored, in macrohistoric circumstance. Conceivably American consciousness and the angle of its relation to the modern world have been affected as much by great historical actions that did not reach the American shore or were not participated in directly as by those endured and circumstantially

4

There is of course a deflecting temptation in all such theorizing (a temptation confirming, perhaps, the very distemper that is to be identified and interpreted). It is the temptation not simply to cramp the historical data into too narrow an explanatory frame but to misconceive and misrepresent their fundamental mode of existence within actual societies, actual history. All art, as Pasternak said, is more one-sided than people think; and however determined (or self-determining) literary history may appear to hindsight, it is like other kinds of history in being more accident-prone, and more incalculable, than—just at present—either its scholar-guardians or its de-mystifiers are disposed to allow. The living community of literature is never identical with society as a whole. One of the real lacunae in contemporary literary theory is an orderly understanding, or even a clear exploratory idea, of this jagged relation; an understanding of how, in brief, the subsociety engaged in serious literary production—the people who read as well as the people who write—maintains and renews itself and establishes whatever canons of preference contrive to dominate the next era. In particular the volatile mix of popular and esoteric influences at work in anything generously creative tends to escape critical accounting, and does so in roughly the same degree as it surprises established expectations: a paradigm nicely exemplified by the performative originality and, coincidentally, muddled critical reception of *Moby-Dick*, of *Huckleberry Finn*, and of *The Waste Land* (to cite instances of unimpeachable importance).

This elusiveness in the character of the genuinely new-made and enlivening is something to keep in mind in any effort to calculate future developments—a questionable effort at best but an uncomfortably natural one. Assumptions persist, for example, that the chief threat to a literature of serious social and moral consequence derives from the vulgarizations of a popular culture backed by the whole weight of modern commercial programming and possessing now an electronically magnified power to lower standards and subvert imaginative judgment. Certainly our late twentieth-century sociotechnical order offers a free field for the proliferating aggres-

---

commemorated. Two such events, profoundly determining on their own ground, are the English civil wars of 1640–60 and, at the start of the industrial age, the wars of the French Revolution. To have missed direct engagement in these convulsions and in the compromises they exacted—an exemption made possible by an extraordinary geopolitical isolation and security—has at the least made it harder through most of our century to outgrow the American propensity to simplistic historical judgments and single-vision solutions.

sions of shoddy workmanship and sheer bad taste. All the same, one may reasonably doubt whether in the United States the over-all social framework which—these are Proust's succinct terms for the issue in question—"supports an art and certifies its authenticity" is now any more in hostage to meretricious excitements than it was in the age (Hawthorne's, Whitman's) of family-magazine sentimentalism and frenzied popular religious revivals, or the age (Dreiser's, Edith Wharton's) of a vaudevillized theater, the yellow press, and the newly invented cinema's narcotic seductions.

In any case, complaints about vulgarization are pointless if they rise in the first place from sheer unresponsiveness, or from a self-approving indifference to such unexpected openings to originality and fresh expressive power as materialized around 1960, notwithstanding mountains of dross, in both *nouvelle vague* filmmaking and the improvised collaborations and adaptations of a mass-marketed popular music: Bob Dylan, the Beatles, Jimi Hendrix, for starters. If a serious art were ever to sustain itself out of this commercialized hurly-burly—as Shakespeare's theater inexplicably arose out of the bear garden, amusement park, blood-and-gore sensationalism of popular London culture in the 1580s, in combination with an imported humanism and problematic new science—it would doubtless be troublesome and confusing to accommodate critically. It might well be an art not immediately recognized as offering, in its own opportunistic fashion, life-serving refreshment; an art and literature (as Stephen Spender innocently surmised half a century ago, trying to imagine what might succeed the disintegrating culture of bourgeois liberalism) "of jokes, free association, dream imagery—all the accidents of wit and beauty, childhood and death, which strike us suddenly when we are in the street"; an art as erratic in its contrivances and as desperately salvaged from confusion as may be imagined, yet once again accessible to the combinatory inventiveness of genius, of intensified local collaboration, or of whatever we think it is that in this year and not some other brings forth—to everyone's surprise—a genuinely new voice and new word.

That there are serious and possibly unprecedented obstacles to any such happy development, obstacles deriving from the conjoint globalization and atomization of "postmodern" experience, is no great secret. In the 1990s it would seem that the writer who is to make a genuine difference to the whole cultural estate will need "more than ever"—more even than seemed the case to Henry James when a century earlier he defined this distinctively American need—"to be a master." Yet mastery itself is something our wary new defensiveness has become foundationally suspicious of. Perhaps a reversion to tribalization, an escape from adverse circumstance into self-contained enclaves that have given up any effort to speak for the common condition— ethnic or feminist enclaves, specialized occupational subgroups converging for self-security upon the workshop concerns that once bound together artisanal communities, even university campuses if everything else fails— will continue to support whatever degree of realization remains in prospect for writers of the era ahead. In some such fashion, in recent years, both talented younger authors and others less young have managed to find audiences sufficient to keep them going: Toni Morrison as well as Grace Paley and Philip Roth, Brad Leithauser as well as John Ashbery and Adrienne Rich. So with some gallantry, and risk, Frank O'Hara did among the New York painters and dancers as well as fellow poets of the 1950s and 1960s, and so too—well short of his most grandiose ambition but securely enough to have compiled an indispensable contemporary record—has Norman Mailer, the last American author to think it natural and reasonable to devote himself on something like a national scale to "making a revolution in the consciousness of our time."

In any such conjecture the moment of utterance leaves its mark. By common consent the present moment in American writing is not a grandly distinguished one. In the long wake of the modernist renaissance there is a broad range of technical competence and much in the way of engaging, if disposable, performative virtuosity; new writers from formerly closed-off ethnic enclaves and cultural subgroups (Chinese Americans, black women) have successfully laid claim to a wide popular hearing; but perhaps only the more or less traditional realism of novelists like John Updike (in the *Rabbit* tetralogy) and latterly Russell Banks (*Continental Drift*) and Don DeLillo (*White Noise, Libra*), and again Norman Mailer in *Harlot's Ghost*, still reaches for something like a classic fullness of representation. Otherwise, in our literature's attenuations of emotion and purpose—its diminished characterizations, its prevailing flatness of idiom, its forced or borrowed ingenuities of design, its retreat from full imaginative mastery—it might well be compared with the closing years of the last century, when, through the 1880s and 1890s, the generation of Emerson, Melville, and Whitman fell silent, gifted younger talents died insufficiently tested (like Stephen Crane) or were disappointingly realized (like Howells), the art of poetry was the preserve of Edmund Clarence Stedman, Joaquin Miller, James Whitcomb Riley, and a few better-tutored but equally conventional college aesthetes and hearties, while figures as masterly as Mark Twain and Henry James seemed (from some points of view: magazine editors, the book-buying public) to be forgetting year by year how to negotiate a fully compelling art of extended prose fiction. Who then would have predicted what the years between 1900 and 1945—from *Sister Carrie*, *The Wings of the Dove*, *Three Lives*, *Personae*, *North of Boston*, *Spring and All*, to *The Sound and the Fury*, *The Bridge*, *U.S.A.*, *Four Quartets*, *Notes Toward a Supreme Fiction*, *The Iceman Cometh*, *Native Son*—were conspiring to bring to pass?

PART II

2

"The People's Author"

Attempting to Find Mr. Mark Twain

[*This essay began life as a talk at Washington University, St. Louis, in 1985, at a symposium sponsored jointly by the university and the Mark Twain Banks consortium to celebrate the sesquicentennial of Twain's birth and the centennial of* The Adventures of Huckleberry Finn. *I began with a comment on the three allusions contained in my title and subtitle. Those in the subtitle were hardly obscure; I assumed that readers of* Huckleberry Finn *would not have forgotten the "Author's Notice" threatening dire consequences to anyone "attempting to find" moral, motive, or plot in what followed—and would remember, too, the opening sentences: "You don't know about me without you have read a book by the name of* The Adventures of Tom Sawyer, *but that ain't no matter. That book was made by Mr. Mark Twain. . . ." But my main title needed explaining. Simply, it was as "the People's Author" that with the runaway success in 1869 of* The Innocents Abroad *Mark Twain's early publisher, Elisha Bliss of Hartford,*

Connecticut, set about consolidating the fast-rising reputation of his star commodity, the new linchpin of his subscription publishing business. That huckster's label set Mark Twain as much apart from other noteworthy men and women of letters, around 1870, as the subscription system itself—the door-to-door retailing of a new book direct from printing house to its families of prospective readers across the nation—was set apart from the respectable book trade. How Elisha Bliss's brash claim was confirmed over the next decade and a half became my organizing theme.]

There has been from the first a considerable elusiveness about Mr. Mark Twain, the famous American writer—about, precisely, his standing and character *as* a writer; about his evident differences from other indubitably important writers (that is, if he was in any orthodox sense a writer of literature); and about the weight, range, and force of significance that can be assigned to the peculiar products of his working life and career. Who indeed was this author, Mr. Mark Twain, and what did he have to say to us, the "people" he wrote for and was publicly advertised, from early on, as writing for? Both during and after his lifetime one of Mark Twain's great services to the republic of letters has been his power of resistance to organized critical scrutiny and the bluff affront his work offers, and continues to offer, to schooled understanding. It is an affront that registers as sharply in our own multiplying commentaries and rationalizations as in the notorious condescension of cultivated opinion while he was alive and writing.

We all know how it is, and how it has been from the beginning, with *Huckleberry Finn* itself. The book is somehow our masterwork in the grand genre of prose fiction; only *Moby-Dick* rivals it as a single text; and if there has been a more densely and continuously "American" book that nevertheless the rest of the world reads and treasures, we are challenged to name it. Yet *Huckleberry Finn* is, as a novel, scandalously slapdash and improvised in execution. For extended passages and sometimes whole episodes it can seem—as it has to many discriminating readers—unhappily at odds with its own peculiar genius. Hemingway's famous judgment in the 1930s, that all modern American writing of any consequence derives from one book in particular, Mark Twain's *Huckleberry Finn*, but that you must skip the last eleven of its forty-three chapters, or one-fourth of the printed text—that much-quoted judgment was in fact anticipated in the earliest reviews. The Boston critic Thomas Sergeant Perry, reviewing *Huckleberry Finn* for *The Century Magazine* in 1885, was only the first of its readers to raise objections to those final chapters and to the whole business of bringing Tom Sawyer back into the story and allowing him to take over, as he largely does, the long closing episode.

This element of critical scandal and effrontery as regards both the author and his best book remains massively unresolved in critical discussion, though many solutions and explanations have been offered. Accordingly I have thought it might be of at least passing interest to apply to it, and to the general problem of "Mr. Mark Twain" and his peculiar legacy, certain propositions which the latest seaswell of critical theorizing has deposited on our shores. Literary criticism in general, as is well known, has been for some time in a state of speculative turmoil and excitement, to the point of radically undermining not only this or that creative reputation or critical practice but of challenging and subverting the very idea of literature itself as traditionally conceived and talked about. A great effort of demystifying, deprivileging, and otherwise deconstructing existing assumptions about literary meanings and values has been going forward—in the academy, at least—for some twenty-five years now, and from this turbulent incursion of *nouvelle critique* (a handy name for it all which acknowledges its conspicuously though not exclusively French provenance), I will pull out three basic critical and metacritical propositions that seem to me to bear with some piquancy on the particular case of Mr. Mark Twain.

The first of these propositions is that there is really no such thing as a *work* of literature—if we mean by that a deliberated construct that in its design and delivered meanings (1) is self-contained, (2) is fully coherent, or embodies a coherent set of performative intentions, and (3) moves purposefully from a definite opening to an equally definite termination, as would, say, a coded message or a project in engineering. Consequently, instead of speaking of literary *works*, we should speak only of *texts*—texts which might begin anywhere, end nowhere, and prove effectively random, or at best self-contradictory, in their internal assemblage. Better yet, we should speak simply of *écriture*, of writing. In this view there are no fully accomplished and self-cohering works of literature. There is only writing, which begins and breaks off according to some succession of accidents that has little or nothing to do with principles of form, of controlled authorial structuring.

The second proposition is a sort of corollary of the first. It is that there is really no such thing as an *author*; more precisely, that critical discourse would do well to get rid of the term, and concept, of the author and of authorship as soon as possible. (This of course proves to have its difficulties. You do notice that even the most resolute practitioners of Foucauldian or Barthesian *nouvelle critique* go on speaking of a certain "Flaubert" or a certain "Henry James" as if some such individual generators of *écriture* had once actually existed.) But the objection to the word "author," and to the conceptual ideology lurking behind it, is that it prolongs false notions of literary creativity and hence of textual and, by extension, social authority. What really produces a given literary text is not an individual author with an important-to-distinguish name and important things to say to us. It is rather the totality of organized culture, and in particular it is *language*, that wholly impersonal signifying system which, to begin with, writers do not themselves invent or establish the rules for, which preexists every particular act of writing, and which as a system transcends the statement-making capacity of any one user or temporal community of users. What literature is about, in this view—and what the production of *écriture* essentially signi-fies—is the grand process of linguistic (and textual) self-extension, or, to put it another way, the everlasting struggle between language-as-such and human weakness, human forgetfulness. So considered, every produced text (measured by canons of authorial intention and structural intelligibility) is necessarily a failure, an act of both self-betrayal and betrayal of the whole commonwealth of human expectation. To go on thinking in conventional ways about *authors* and their *works* is to conspire willy-nilly in acts of ontological mystification and potentially repressive false consciousness.

The third proposition is really a cluster of propositions, or theories, and one interesting thing about them is that they essentially contradict the first two, insofar as they require our predicating identifiable producers whose names can be looked up, authors who do compose distinguishable verbal objects that as a reader you can hold in your hands and turn the pages of, from the first block of typographic signifiers to the last. First, insofar as there is an inferable *somebody*, a discoursing subject-presence whose extended activity leads to the appearance of a *something*—a book, poem, story, play, sketch, treatise: a material text, at all events—this new something always enters the historical world it coexists with as an act of provocation and subversion. Literature in this view is always adversarial as regards the habits of mind of the age in which it is produced, and the individual writer (I quote here Professor Geoffrey Hartman) is one who "confronts," who "takes up arms against," the beliefs and prejudices of his age. So each new literary work (in the summary by Professor Hayden White of the provocation theory propounded by Hans Robert Jauss of the Konstanz school of criticism) "figures a way of knowing which conflicts with the ways of knowing" of its era. It challenges the era's values and perceptions, and exposes its casuistries; consequently, "every genuine work of art appears as a revolutionary gesture" and is therefore understood by its first audience as a positive threat, to the moral order if not directly to public safety. As a sort of corollary to this confrontation theory of literature, there is also the theory that—if again there really is something we may call a *work* of literature—its real subject is not its professed theme or ostensible narrative action. Its real subject is the reader. And its meaning is the mind-set, the *mentalité*, the consciousness of its readership; that consciousness without whose active connivance, however obtained, literary meanings cannot be said to exist at all.

Let me quickly say—in case some overtone of satirical dubiety, or amazement, or both, has crept into the foregoing summary—that there is much of value in these views and respectable enough reasons for their currency over the past quarter century. We have all had our wits sharpened by them, if only in being reminded of things we should have known all along—and mostly did know, in other terms. But my concern here is not with sorting out the claims of such theories, or the objections to them, but with seeing whether and how they fit the case of Mr. Mark Twain; whether, in confrontation with them, Mark Twain preserves his record of resisting stringent critical analysis. It strikes me that he does.

2

Consider the second proposition first: that there is really no such thing as an originating author, whose presence *in* the work is the source of whatever it is that holds us *to* the work.[1] Immediately, with Mark Twain, a peculiar situation arises. Who—or what—is it, in this case, that we are to stop thinking about, to consider as nonexistent or as no more than a distinguished absence? To know anything at all about the personage "Mark Twain" is to know that he was as much a fictional creation, a tissue of predicated verbal otherness, as is Pap Finn or Hank Morgan. The man who invented him, one Samuel Langhorne Clemens, brought off throughout his working life an authorial disappearing act far more effective, in actuality, than the one promoted by Paris criticism. (One clear sign of this is that even in Missouri nobody has undertaken to incorporate and keep in business a "Samuel L. Clemens" banking consortium.)

1. To explore the merits of this proposition, there isn't a better place to start than William H. Gass's elegantly witty meditation on Roland Barthes's landmark essay, "The Death of the Author": see "The Death of the Author" in Gass's *Habitations of the Word* (1985).

We also know that in setting up a certain "Mark Twain" as the putative inscriber of the *écriture* that concerns us, Samuel Clemens was following a well-grooved convention of self-displacement, and was recognized by his first readers as doing so. Just as the mid-nineteenth-century Cleveland newspaperman Charles Farrar Browne had become a proper author by disappearing behind a drop-screen called "Artemus Ward," or as the California humorist George Horatio Derby spoke only through a fictive mask labeled "John Phoenix"—both precedents handsomely acknowledged by Twain himself—so Samuel Clemens, when it came to writing, abdicated every day in favor of a whole verbal commonwealth that he denominated "Mark Twain." Moreover, he pledged himself, as he did so, to protect and preserve that commonwealth's expressive treasure. As the whole point of removing the *author* from the field of critical consideration is to stress the absolute dependence of any new utterance on other and earlier utterances, so Twain regularly claimed that he was only recording what had already been said or spoken. He was retelling old tales, giving a fresh turn to episodes and performances that had delighted audiences for decades if not centuries past. If we know only *Huckleberry Finn*, we know the literal truth of this. Precedents and rival versions for set-piece passages like the King's camp-meeting scam, the Duke of Bilgewater's all-purpose Shakespearean soliloquy, or the minstrel-show exchanges between Huck and Jim have been found all over the corpus of mid-nineteenth-century popular entertainment. Even Pap Finn's classic tirade against the gov'ment has its verified precedent in Samuel Clemens's own vernacular outbursts to family and friends in the drawing room of his Hartford mansion.

To have anticipated a later critical theory is not, of course, to have disproved it—rather the contrary—but it is, perhaps, to suggest that the new theory, as formulated, need not require our adopting a totally new critical method and value system. Besides, if there is some danger that impressionable minds might take too literally the "death of the author" idea, who but Mark Twain has already supplied the antidote? We can hear him saying it: reports of this notable contemporary event—the extinction of *authors* as a significant cognitive species—have been considerably exaggerated.

Of the first of these three new-New-Critical notions, that properly speaking there is no such thing as a *work* of literature, less needs to be said here. That a writer can rise to worldwide fame and influence without ever producing a coherent book, Mark Twain is, again, proof positive. At the least he requires us to rethink the basic idea of formal coherence, or of expressive consistency, as supreme aesthetic and performative values. For Mark Twain is that indubitably artful, indubitably consequential writer who—long before our criticism began lisping the impressive foreign word, *clôture*—made it a point of honor to avoid proper narrative closure, to bring nothing longer than a page and a half to strict formal completeness, to market his writings with audiences high and low solely on the basis of his opportunistic command of a long-established popular repertory of anecdotes and tales, freshly reconstituted, and of well-seasoned performative routines; his command, that is, of the abundant resources of popular recollection. It was this popular repertory that, in a favorite metaphor of his, filled and refilled the tank or cistern of his mind and memory. On any given working day, so he said, he had only to make sure the cistern was full again, and then pull the plug and let it flow.

To put the matter another way: Mark Twain may be that early modern writer who most conspicuously anticipates Mikhail Bakhtin's persuasive theory that power and vitality come into narrative prose precisely as it turns dialogic and, indeed, polyphonic—multitongued, multitoned, multipurposed; as it registers not one voice and vision but a whole chorus, if not hodgepodge, of competing voices and visions. Mark Twain practiced an art of dissonance, and flourished within it, long before that quality got inscribed as a first principle of a distinctly modern, and modernist, aesthetic.

But it is the third of these newish critical theories that interests me most in relation to that elusive authorial phenomenon, Mr. Mark Twain; in particular the idea that the work of literature that matters is one that enters history as a challenge and provocation to the settled attitudes of its audience, and as a revolutionary threat to its readers' deepest habits of mind, along with the corollary idea that the audience itself, or the reader, is the work's real subject.

Twain's popularity in his own time goes without saying; and all in all, it seems unlikely that the book-buying public would take to its heart a writer whom it perceived as seriously threatening its own values and attitudes. So we may at this point be reminded of one standard older argument about Mr. Mark Twain. This is the argument (forcefully advanced a decade after his death in Van Wyck Brooks's *The Ordeal of Mark Twain*) that his extraordinary talent was ultimately crippled by the need to keep on good terms with his middle-American public. He might have been, so the argument goes, a satirist of the power, the comprehensive and unconstrained truthfulness, of a Jonathan Swift—or of a Dickens, for that matter. Instead, as mass popularity became indispensable to his image of himself as an author, he effectively interiorized the squeamishness and mediocrity he was surrounded by, and deliberately surrounded himself with (beginning with his *bien pensante* wife and with literary friends and monitors like William Dean Howells—who in fact seem to have been considerably less severe than he was himself in deleting possibly offensive passages). This is an argument that probably is unresolvable, one reason being that it gains rather than loses force from easy-to-assemble biographical and textual evidence that Twain did, repeatedly, walk right up to the boundaries of what was publicly acceptable and hang teasingly around those boundaries, even if he would not finally plant his foot on the other side. Every knowledgeable commentator has sensed Twain's own double-mindedness in this regard, along with the ambiguities and fits of self-disparagement it resulted in, and has sensed in particular a counter-strain of open hostility toward the cultural mores he allegedly surrendered to.

One place to test such findings is in the texts of the innumerable public addresses, speeches, toasts and answers to toasts that, once his mass popularity was secured, Twain was continually on call to deliver. There remains a whole published volume of these performances, where we find him speaking directly to the public that loved him; the public that went on buying his books, as it seems to us, without regard to their intrinsic merit and that now sat in front of him, waiting once again to be entertained. In these addresses, this direct commerce with his proper audience, there is over and over again a nervy approach to something tactless or indecorous or openly offensive. Each time, the sharpness of the fun comes precisely in the speaker's balancing act (which his hearers of course come to anticipate) along the knife edge of provocation and unacceptability.

Some of these occasions became legendary: his speech at a Grand Army of the Republic reunion honoring the great General and retired President U. S. Grant (here Twain describes in mock-epic language Grant's hard-won success at the age of six months, sitting in his crib, in the soldierly task of forcing his big toe up into his wide-open mouth), or the notorious address at the Whittier birthday celebration. This latter occasion, in which the venerable New England priesthood of Longfellow, Emerson, Holmes and all was re-created as a crowd of mining-territory bums and deadbeats, was one that, fairly typically, Mark Twain himself exaggerated the immediate scandal of (if there was any immediate scandal) in order to have the matter both ways. He could wallow abjectly in apologies—someone who knew him well remarked that "his whole life was one long apology"—and at the same time claim injury at the hands of his too thin-skinned listeners, who were not up to an innocent after-dinner joke. Such occasions, and the combination of remorse and resentment the recollection of them produced in him, tended to bring to full boil the whole volatile amalgam of Mark Twain's temperament. Justin Kaplan, in his biography Mr. Clemens and Mark Twain, has summed up as well as anyone who the man himself was who repeatedly landed in trouble of this kind:

> He was excitable, easily hurt, desperately hungry for affection and tenderness, often depressed, capable of great rage and of greater remorse. He remained, in many ways, a child demanding attention in the nursery [though it was, Kaplan nicely adds, a nursery "as large as the world"].

As a single minor instance let me offer a synopsis of what one such occasion was like, and trace out the sequence of borderline insults and provocations that Twain laid on for his immediate audience. This is an address to the New England Society of Philadelphia delivered on December 22, 1881, the two hundred and sixty-first anniversary of the Pilgrims' landing at what became Plimoth Plantation. Twain opens by expressing puzzlement and, indeed, considerable irritation at the affair itself. He demands of his audience, "What do you want to celebrate those people for," that hoary old "Mayflower tribe"? What is there to celebrate in the simple fact that they landed and came ashore? If they hadn't landed—in the middle of winter, in a snowstorm, wet and battered from weeks at sea—that might be worth commemorating. It would in fact have been a case of "monumental leather-headedness." Of course (he at once goes on to say) "if it had been you, gentlemen, you probably wouldn't have landed."

Also, there's the fact that one can't even be sure what precisely is being celebrated. "One of you says it's the landing. The other says it's the Pilgrims," and this is characteristic: "You Boston people never do agree about anything—except the importance of Boston." Nevertheless (he concedes), perhaps there is something to celebrate after all. No doubt they were, those Pilgrims, a better lot than a good many of their forebears in history—though this isn't anything to boast about. There is always some progress from generation to generation, and no doubt you, their descendants, are in turn an improvement of sorts. "Yes," he says, to this admiring audience of businessmen, lawyers, doctors, "those among you who have not been in the penitentiary, if such there be, are no doubt better than your fathers and grandfathers were"—and then another jab—"but that's no reason for getting up annual dinners celebrating you."

No, Twain continues, a truer celebration would be one honoring *my* first American ancestor, who happened to be an Indian. And how did your ancestors treat him? They "skinned him alive, and thus I am an orphan." You ought to celebrate *him*—and you ought to do it in the right costume, which of course would be no clothes at all. (The chance to give Victorian prurience a titillating suggestion of undiscussable alternatives was rarely missed.) In full stride now Twain also claims various New England Quakers among his ancestry, people his audience's ancestors flogged and then ran out of town. There were also those Salem witches you tried and hanged; they, too, were "ancestors of mine"—and for a giddy moment a historical revisionism as sweeping as Brooks Adams's or Charles Beard's comes into view, a fundamental rewriting of America's beautiful history from the point of view not of its self-satisfied inheritors and beneficiaries but of its long trail of summary victims.

Characteristically the address retreats from this historical realism back into comic extravagance. Looking about him and noting that his audience is drinking punch and lemonade and may soon descend, if this keeps up, to tea or, worse yet, to coffee (and hotel coffee at that), Twain launches into a general call to reform. "Disband," he cries, "these New England societies," these "perpetuators of ancestral superstition." "Renounce these soul-blistering saturnalia; cease from varnishing the rusty reputations of your long-vanished ancestors—the super-high-moral old iron-clads of Cape Cod, the pious buccaneers of Plymouth Rock." "Go home, and try to learn to behave!"—a recommendation followed by a final paragraph in which Twain recalls a grandfather of his who once declared that "it would be pretty hard to improve on those people" (the old Pilgrim stock), and then, shifting into his down-home drawl, "as for me, I don't mind coming out flatfooted and saying, there ain't any way to improve on them—except having them born in Missouri." All in good fun, but with an edge to it nevertheless, or just enough of an edge to make one regret his not breaking free altogether into a more telling challenge to upper-class American filiopietism.

3

But it is in the main sequence of his published writings that Mark Twain's relation to his readership needs to be tested, and in the space remaining I want to look, all too hastily, at the run of books that first won him his popular standing, as regards the proposition that what they embody is a comprehensive and by no means flattering diagnosis of the society and readership that came to honor him with an unshakeable affection. The core trick in all these earlier books is the same rhetorical double-mindedness that brings off the speech to the New England Society, but now writ large and elaborately sustained. A triple-mindedness, actually, since it encompasses (1) the declared subject of the book; (2) the putative consciousness of those who are to receive this account of the subject (who, literally, will subscribe to it); and (3) the equally implicated consciousness, the writer's own, that stage-manages the whole performance. It is above all this third component that, in its variousness and indeed inconsistency, repeatedly charges the texts that result with the backbite of a reassuringly self-inclusive irony. The briefs of condemnation Twain filed with his public differ in this fundamental respect from the anathemas distributed by his western-American successor Ezra Pound; they are not (as Eliot remarked of Pound's conception of hell) reserved exclusively for other people. If there is an argument in these books with (or against) the spirit and character of the age, there is a not less sharply joined argument within the writer's own imagination; and it has a greater force precisely as the writer's imagination does not distance itself from that spirit and character but essentially reproduces it.

Interestingly, if we go back to the earliest reviews, we find that some at least among Twain's first readers were aware of the satirical complications in his narrative art; and in case anyone should miss this third part of it, this element of self-reference and self-chastisement, Twain himself was on hand to fill them in. Of course, some of those who commented on *The Innocents Abroad* seemed to have missed every part of it, or saw only that the idealizations of conventional travel writing had been turned upside down. It wasn't only a question of not recognizing the well-seasoned tricks of a specifically American brand of humor. A British critic's remark that *Innocents Abroad* "sets a slur upon all the beauty and splendor" lying in its author's path can be matched by a stiff-necked American comment that the book was, all in all, a "masterpiece of vulgarity."

But other reviewers, on both sides of the water, saw clearly enough that *The Innocents Abroad*'s real subject was not Europe at all, and the monuments and splendors of her glorious or sacred past. It was, as the title plainly declared, the American travelers and cultural pilgrims. (Readers will recall that Twain's subtitle for the book was "The New Pilgrim's Progress.") Above all, it was the combination of ignorance, vanity, touchiness, and impenetrable self-complacency with which these new pilgrims, these imperial selves, marched and sailed across the ancient world. Howells's review for the *Atlantic Monthly* went straight to the mark in noticing that the author had got the larger part of his fun in the book from observing and giving voice to his fellow passengers; Bret Harte (still at this point on friendly though patronizing terms with Twain) compared him to other satirists who find their best targets within their own circle, "among their own best friends." A dozen years later, looking back at all of Twain's work to date, Thomas Sergeant Perry returned to the same point. "What is *Innocents Abroad*," Perry wrote, "but a full account of the raw unregenerate American character?"—highlighted in this case by being set loose in a grander world. "What *is* the state of mind of that American but *contempt* for what he sees, and an infinite self-satisfaction?" Yet the American state of mind evoked in the narrative is, we may assume, the same state of mind that hugely enjoyed reading about these things—which is to say, reading about itself, at this one slight remove.

To this account of Twain's basic strategy in *Innocents Abroad* may be added the findings of those scholars who have compared in detail the texts of his original letters from Europe to the San Francisco and New York papers with the transformed text of the book itself. What he had done, from start to finish, was to transfer the lampooning, in the newspaper letters, of a fictitious fellow pilgrim named "Brown," who never understands what he is looking at, back onto his own authorial shoulders. Perhaps it was from a sense that his readers hadn't fully grasped this transformation-from-within that Twain, in an anonymous followup review that he wrote himself, zeroed in on the narrative *persona* he had created, and had meant to create, particularizing in this narrator "his insolence, impertinence, presumption, mendacity, and above all majestic ignorance."

Three years later, with the all-American setting of *Roughing It* (1872), Mark Twain's representation of his fellow countrymen, and by implication of the mass of his readership, became a full compass point more direct. Twain himself described *Roughing It* as "a book about America," a characterization mediated of course by the peculiar excitements of mining-camp life out West. What we may remember best from *Roughing It* are a whole set of self-contained comic, or farcical, episodes and descriptive cadenzas. Who will forget the soliloquy attributed to the Mormon patriarch Brigham Young on the burdens of everyday domestic life, with eighty or ninety children clamoring for equal attention, not to mention the older ones who are "off at college," and with nine hundred and eighty-four separate pieces of laundry to be done every week; a soliloquy that ends with a precise description of the patriarch's bedstead, seven feet long and ninety-six feet wide. Who forgets the long coyote-versus-dog anecdote—the makers of our road-runner cartoon series did not forget it—or the careless devastation by fire, in a sort of end-of-the-world burn-up, of the shoreline of magnificent Lake Tahoe?

But what also steadily emerges through all the separate episodes in *Roughing It* is something for which "subtext" is too weak a term. It is nothing less than a panoramic vision of an entire national society caught up in a hallucinatory epidemic of greedy acquisitiveness, all its ordinary relationships reduced by the gold fever to a cut-throat scramble for quick fortunes. The book's matter-of-fact representation of the way in which people actually treat each other in the world of the narrative thus stands as a vision, or nightmare, of modern American life as a whole. And once again Twain's narrative strategy is to make this national story his own story as well, as he rapidly becomes a consenting accomplice in the historical action he describes; as he, too, falls victim to the same fever of acquisition. It was a strategy that carried over into the first version of the Hawaiian Islands chronicle he subsequently attached to the end of *Roughing It*, to fill it out to subscription-book length: the 1869 platform lecture which had borne the title, "Our Fellow Savages of the Sandwich Islands."

With the novel *The Gilded Age* in 1873, the compass needle of, at once, a national and a personal self-diagnosis moves another point or two nearer the center. The narrative voice in *The Gilded Age* shifts into the third person, as befits the book's full-dress attack not only on the American political establishment—the corruption by economic greed of the entire political and institutional system—but also upon the population, the national constituency, which both tolerates this corruption and actively connives in it. Twain himself is mordantly present in the book (or in his part of it; he wrote it in collaboration with a forgotten Connecticut author, Charles Dudley Warner). Certainly it is Twain's voice we hear in the acerbic twenty-fourth chapter describing Washington, D.C., as it looked to an outsider half a decade past the Civil War; but he is, in *The Gilded Age*, even more memorably present in the larger-than-life figure of Colonel Beriah Sellers, who epitomizes both a whole society's eager capacity for self-delusion and Mark Twain's own prodigal appetite for promotional daydreaming. In Colonel Sellers, Howells privately told Twain, you have created "the American character" for our time. Details of this characterization derive from Twain's observation of a scatterbrained cousin of his on his mother's side, but the imaginative knowledge sustaining it is, first of all, self-knowledge.

Curiously, when after *The Gilded Age* Twain began as a writer to draw on his own earliest memories and to pour forth those pre–Civil War recollections that are the source of what came to be considered his finest writing, he suffered a distinct falling off in popularity. *The Adventures of Tom Sawyer*, in 1876, found its public at a markedly slower rate than the books that preceded it; during its first year in print *Tom Sawyer* sold barely twenty thousand copies, whereas the first-year sales of *Innocents Abroad* had run to nearly seventy thousand. But the complex of Twain's purposes hadn't really changed. Howells, in any case, saw *Tom Sawyer* as a direct continuation of his essential work as chronicler of the national life. "The whole little town of St. Petersburg," Howells wrote in the *Atlantic*, "is brought to life for the reader"—and Howells's list of features is an interesting one—"in its religiousness, its lawlessness, its droll social distinctions [a commonly underrated aspect of *Tom Sawyer*], its civilization qualified by slave-holding, and its Wild-West trace." A review in the *Times* of London laid special emphasis on a certain "republican freedom from class prejudice" among the book's gang of boys; an aspect of the story so familiar and natural-seeming to its American readers as virtually to escape notice.

4

But it is with *The Adventures of Huckleberry Finn* that, like any self-respecting account of Mark Twain, this one will come to an end. My closing proposition is simply that the peculiar power and authority of *Huckleberry Finn* are directly related to the peculiar intimacy of its contacts with both the mind of its audience and the mind of its prodigal-son creator. The problems of judgment that the book still presents us with are a clear reflection of this: problems that in the 1980s and 1990s have made it once again as controversial a text for public-school committees and syllabus preparers as it famously was in 1885 for the Concord, Massachusetts, library committee, which refused to stock it.

Again, the book's best early readers did understand, rather better than Twain himself, its singular imaginative authority. One journalistic notion that had occupied readers and reviewers all through the first twenty years of Twain's career was a notion summed up in the title of an 1868 essay for the new *Nation* magazine by the Connecticut novelist John W. DeForest, an essay called, proleptically, "The Great American Novel." American writers, it was implied, had a positive duty to produce such a work—one that would offer a "tableau of American society" as a whole; that would portray "the ordinary emotions and manners of American existence" yet give "national breadth to the picture"; in sum, a single tale that would paint American life "so broadly, truly, and sympathetically, that every American will be forced to acknowledge it as a true likeness." To DeForest, only *Uncle Tom's Cabin*, with its focus on a great issue of national politics and with characters drawn from every geographical section of the country, had so far approached this status. Over the next two decades there were plenty of candidates—*The Gilded Age* was one; Henry James's *The American*, in its parabolic fashion, was another—but it was left to an alert foreign critic, Andrew Lang, to point out (six years after *Huckleberry Finn*) that the much-discussed "great American novel" had now appeared, though it had "escaped the eyes of those who were watching for it." In *Huckleberry Finn*, Lang wrote in 1891, we have a novel that in historicist perspective is more valuable than *Uncle Tom's Cabin*, being (among other virtues) uncluttered by partisan purposes.

If we do take the book as a representation of the whole national life moving in its most intimate history, we have to acknowledge that *Huckleberry Finn* is distinctly less flattering than the "hymn to boyhood" Mark Twain claimed to have written in *Tom Sawyer*. The action of *Tom Sawyer* has its share of violence and terror, but for the most part these are subordinated to a certain nostalgic optimism about the general course of St. Petersburg life. Moments of violence and terror serve mainly as reminders that an extravagant fearfulness is as normal to American childhood as are high jinks and an egalitarian freedom of behavior. The world of *Huckleberry Finn*, once the story gets going, is another matter. Various events that mark the main story of *Tom Sawyer*—a knife murder, the single drowning, threats of vengeance and mutilation, a death by starvation in a sealed cave—open out in *Huckleberry Finn* into a proper carnival of drowning and killing, threatened lynching, armed posses, feuds that last for generations and wipe out whole families, and an actual tar-and-feathering. Moreover, the tale is told this time by a narrator who, though he is sometimes sickened by these events, repeatedly accepts them as simply the way of the world.

Certainly Huck himself, or Mark Twain's use of him to tell this story of a world he never made, is decisive to the book's peculiar greatness. This is our common critical wisdom about it: that in turning over the telling of the story to a character who tells it in the very accent and idiom of the popular world the book surveys yet himself has no place in that world, wanting nothing from it except to be left alone, Mark Twain found his own best voice as a writer. Of course he is *in* Huck himself, a good deal more substantially than he was in *The Gilded Age*'s Colonel Sellers. The great sustaining dream of pursuit and escape that holds the book together—of a helpless attraction to the human world that sprawls out along the banks of the great river, and of an ultimate betrayal by that world—is Mark Twain's own lifelong dream, and nightmare. So, too, is that most familiar of narrative climaxes in Twain's fiction, the fantasy of a single astonishing theatrical coup bringing about a sudden personal reversal of fortune, perhaps even of personal—and public—identity. But in *Huckleberry Finn* this transforming moment, this quite classical *peripeteia*, outdoes all those others that are triumphantly acclaimed by flabbergasted crowds; outdoes them in being performed, this once, altogether in secret. No one but Huck himself (and the reader) hears him say—in what not long ago I found yet another American author calling the greatest single dramatic moment in our literature—"All right, then, I'll *go* to hell."

Yet if Mark Twain is in Huck himself, he is also intimately inside all the other memorable moments and figures in the narrative. Certainly some part of him is in the King and the Duke and their schemes for making money out of an infinitely gullible public; he is in Colonel Sherburn's scornful putdown of the village lynch mob, and inside Buck Harkness's shamefaced retreat as well; he is in Mrs. Judith Loftus's clever penetration of Huck's disguise as Sarah Mary Williams George Elexander Peters; there is another renegade part of him in the communal babble of old Sister Hotchkiss, Sister Utterback and company (who provide one of several reasons why I, for one, refuse to throw out those last eleven chapters). Above all, I would want to insist, Mr. Mark Twain is inside the character of Pap Finn, the more so as Pap Finn is himself the embodiment of all the classic vices and prejudices of the mass American populace—the insularity, the social envy and rancor, the racism, the shiftlessness and drunkenness that as far back as William Byrd of Westover in the early eighteenth century have been identified as one unarguable result of the historic American experiment in material and social freedom.

The character and in particular the speeches given to Pap Finn bring us directly up against the much controverted matter of the book's treatment of its black characters. That is a subject in itself, not something to be tossed off in a final paragraph. (I will acknowledge that it has become harder and harder to accommodate, in reading *Huckleberry Finn*, the repeated casual use of the word "nigger," despite all the sound critical reasons that can be given for its narratological acceptability.) Here all that needs to be said is that though the slave Jim is the first American black to be presented, by a white author, as a major character on exactly the same plane of moral heroism as the book's white protagonist, he is also, to Mark Twain, a figure of fun; a figure out of the rankest traditions of bug-eyed darky comedy. In a way not really all that different from Pap Finn, Mark Twain himself would have found something fairly grotesque in the apparition of a freed slave with a gold watch and silver-headed cane who was a professor of foreign languages in some holier-than-thou Ohio college. (The difference, of course, is that Mark Twain, or rather Samuel Clemens, wouldn't have physically shoved the man out of his way, if he'd met him, on a public sidewalk.) So, too, Pap Finn's diatribe against a gov'ment that permits such absurdities, and at the same time deprives *him* of his worldly rights, has the ring of an entire authenticity, in the literal sense of the word. Its populist rancor is, again, Mark Twain's own. It is the vibrant underside of his aristocratic, indeed imperial, self-image, and of that genuine though fitfully projected nobility of spirit that led Howells to memorialize him as "the Lincoln of our literature."

Who then is Mr. Mark Twain? He is many things, bless him, but one central thing he is from first to last, as a writer, is our great master of populist resentment, or *ressentiment*—only Faulkner, in the Jason section of *The Sound and the Fury*, can fully match him—and in speaking of *ressentiment*, which some political theorists have called the master motive of all modern mass politics, we are speaking of a political emotion and force that threatens more than ever to dominate both our domestic history and the turbulences that challenge national policy all across the world. It is on this ground, I think, that Mark Twain converges most directly with his enduring American readership. If he remains in some deep sense a challenge and provocation, it is only that nothing he confronts us with, or compels us to acknowledge, goes beyond what our own collective fantasies and night-mares—and our occasional moments of clear-sighted self-scrutiny—have challenged us to recognize in ourselves.

Of Mr. Mark Twain, then, we may finally say that he served our still-struggling-to-be-democratic commonwealth in the best way imaginable; he gave point and substance in his writing to a free people's continuous though largely unreflective argument with itself. What Edwin Muir once beautifully said of Yeats and his relation to living audiences fits Mark Twain as well:

that in regularly creating in his writing a role for himself and in playing that role to the hilt, he presented to his public "a great faulty image, in which they [might] find their own faults and their own hidden greatness. . . ." In Mark Twain's case, as I hope to have suggested, not so very hidden after all.

3

Emily Dickinson

The Community of the Poem

[As the opening talk at a sesquicentennial gathering at Brooklyn College in December 1980, the text that follows (which I have let stand in conversational form) predicated a certain loss of focus in the most recent Dickinson commentaries, a sliding off from the appeal of the poetry itself into psychoanalytic or deconstructionist or new-feminist speculations largely programmed in advance, or else into what Gérard Genette has called paratextual matters (orthography, the arrangement of the poems into bound fascicles, probable datings, and so forth). Since then, things have, to casual observation, shown marked improvement. At the risk of unfairness to the generality of recent work, two studies in particular seem to me to deserve special mention: Christopher Benfey's Emily Dickinson and the Problem of Others (1984), supporting its readings with a philosophic alertness to the issues of skepticism and privacy and with a shrewd critical understanding of lyric obliquity, and Helen McNeil's Emily Dickinson (1986), *in particular the chapter "The Spoken and the Written," emphasizing historically changing conventions of social discourse.*]

Generating subtlety after critical subtlety, the attraction Emily Dickinson continues to exert over our criticism's inquisitorial restlessness confirms judgments of her essential strength and integrity. Yet this magnetizing sense of some still unsorted reserve of poetic authority has also worked to make critical commentary increasingly microscopic, pushing off to the margins certain commonplace considerations that remain indispensable to any ac‑ curate reading of her singular and (be it admitted) still problematic achieve‑ ment. My title for this essay is meant rather literally to evoke one such governing consideration; the immediate practical context and local circum‑ stance of her poetry's emergence. What I have in mind divides two ways— but these are not at all unrelated.

By "the community of the poem" I mean, first, the human and historical community that Emily Dickinson of Amherst, Massachusetts, grew up within during the early‑middle nineteenth century and that, as it fostered a particular apprehension of life, directly nourished both her imaginative outlook and her distinctive habit of expression. About this community— family, town, cultural province—much has been written in the years since her poetry became known, and on the whole it has proved of cardinal value in reaching a more discriminating understanding; the more so since as Emily Dickinson's life advanced she herself was less and less inclined to offer circumstantial explanations. One way of characterizing this historical com‑ munity—in which during the 1830s and 1840s the old religious conscious‑ ness, however dispersed and attenuated, was still a potent energizing force— would be to borrow the phrase Emerson once used in drawing up an account of his "advantages" as a writer, when he summed them all up as, simply, "the total New England." It seems reasonable to assume that Dickinson had in mind much the same set of inherited advantages when she described her own settled vocation as "seeing New Englandly."

If we look back to earlier commentaries on her verse, especially to the serious and intense criticism that gathered around it in the thriving New‑ Critical epoch of the 1920s and 1930s, we notice how regularly, in explain‑ ing her wit and power, appeal is made to the poet's good fortune in inheriting the older New England sensibility at precisely the historical moment when all its original premises—spiritual, civil, existential; literary, too—had been thrown radically into question. Allen Tate's essay of 1932 offers a compact version of this argument: Emily Dickinson was born and came of age exactly at the point of final divergence between an old and a new cultural order when, nevertheless, a degree of equilibrium still obtained between them. Puritanism, Tate wrote, could not be to her what it had been to the generation of Cotton Mather, a body of unassailable truth. It remained, however, a discipline of mind exquisitely attuned to the temper and pulse of her inner life.

But also—and this is the second way of construing my title—I have in mind the more specialized question of whom precisely these poems were written to, or for. What reader or (better) listener and direct recipient was imagined for them? And what community of listeners do they, by their very existence, appear to assume? One thing we know for certain about them is that they were not regularly being dispatched to the editors of *Poetry: A Magazine of Verse, The Hudson Review, The New Yorker,* or to any forerunner of these journals, nor were they written to be carried about for use on college-campus reading tours—though we also know that more than once she did solicit for them the attention of an eminent magazine personage, T. W. Higginson of the new *Atlantic Monthly,* and that a handful did get into print during her lifetime.

To phrase this second consideration in a way that leads more directly to the heart of the matter: in the economy of Emily Dickinson's writing what part is to be played—and is meant to be played—by a reader, an auditor?[1] Exploring the question in this form, we begin to discover some remarkably different answers to it. Here is the unfailingly discerning and suggestive R. P. Blackmur, writing in 1937. We must remember, Blackmur admonishes us, that Dickinson was "a private poet"—"private" in the particular sense of being altogether indifferent to what, in the Eliotized era when Blackmur was writing, critics of poetry were in the habit of calling "the tradition"—and that she paid the price in poetic coherence and intelligibility for being so. The specifically poetic effectiveness of her work was therefore, with regard to the art and practice of poetry, accidental, and this is as true of her moments of triumph as it is of her performative negligences and eccentricities; her failures, Blackmur remarks (on the whole forgivingly), were as

---

1. Giving this form to the question may sound suspiciously fashionable. Reader-oriented criticism is currently in full flood: a predictable response, I suspect, on the part of commentators who are also classroom teachers, to a classroom situation in which even at Harvard College and the University of Konstanz most of one's students are reading, and hearing, poems for very nearly the first time, and one discovers that virtually nothing in the way of contributory information or preparation can be counted on.

On the other hand, beginning with Aristotle, what intelligent critical theory, and theory of literature generally, has not been, among other things, audience-oriented?

accidental as her successes. And her reader is required first of all to adjust to the consequences of this fact. "No poet of anything like her accomplishment," Blackmur concluded, "has ever imposed on the reader such varied and continuous critical labor." Some years later F. O. Matthiessen took up the same theme in his preface to a new *Oxford Book of American Verse*; for its devoted reader not less than for the textual scholar proposing to edit it properly, Emily Dickinson's work presents "all the peculiar problems of the private poet."

Yet we can turn to the equally discerning Northrop Frye and find him saying, apparently, just the opposite. In Frye's view Emily Dickinson was "a genuinely popular poet who quickly found her own public," and found it "in spite of what the highbrows were saying." (The highbrows in this instance were Victorian belletrists like Thomas Bailey Aldrich and Andrew Lang who dismissed Emily Dickinson as "uneducated.") But "private" and "popular" are not necessarily antithetical as critical terms, and I would argue that both views, Blackmur's and Frye's, are essentially true; each is grounded in historically accurate conceptions of the uses of poetry and of the cultural function of major literature. They do not so much contradict each other as point, here, to something peculiar in the whole case Emily Dickinson presents as a figure in literary history: a problematic case, to repeat, yet not more so than that of a good many other indispensable literary figures—such as, for one, her great popular contemporary Mark Twain, another famous and willful violator of belletristic proprieties, and producer of more than one critically exasperating masterpiece.

Some well-established statistical facts are in order here, to keep us on a straight course. We know, for example, that all of Emily Dickinson's nearly eighteen hundred distinguishable poems did not have the same original standing in her own mind or represent the same intensity of purpose. At least half were, literally, occasional poems, or started out that way: poems written to accompany a private letter, a holiday gift, a message of thanks or condolence. Or they were, in considerable proportion, cross-lots communications within her immediate family. The estimate is that fully three hundred of the poems that survive were sent directly as messages to her sister-in-law, Susan Gilbert Dickinson, an auditor and recipient who, for all the biographical animus she has inspired, appears to have been receptive to poetic communication—so Emily Dickinson herself believed—to a degree that brother Austin, Susan's husband, was not. On such circumstantial facts hang fundamental issues of judgment and understanding. One instance in particular has been widely noted: poem #1400 in the Johnson edition, with its climactic stanzas about "nature" as being, for the poet, a ghostly presence, a "haunted" house, and about being oneself estranged from nature and essentially baffled by it the closer it is approached. But in what appears to be the first written-out version, the verse reads not "nature" but "Susan"—it is Susan's house that is "haunted," Susan who is "a stranger yet," Susan whose friends and intimates "know her less / The nearer her they get"—at which point interpretation is only one of the issues forcing itself on critical attention. There is also the established fact (though it remains hermeneutically unresolvable) that roughly half of Emily Dickinson's numbered production consists of poems which she herself arranged and sewed up in packets and did not specifically designate to be destroyed after her death.

We need, in brief, to keep in mind the differences between at least these two basic kinds of poem, the occasional and the more intensely deliberated—at the same time not forgetting to enjoy both kinds, and to enjoy them according to their communicative kind. We need also to notice corresponding differences, or changes of voice, within individual poems. I remember hearing the poet Anthony Hecht give wonderfully precise emphasis to this latter eccentricity of Emily Dickinson's verse-making by reading aloud poem #328, "A Bird came down the Walk—", and showing, as he read, how this little backyard allegory, just kept back from whimsicality in the opening stanzas by the characteristic reminder that backyard birds are, after all, carnivores and kin to dragons, suddenly turns breathcatchingly visionary and original. The warily greedy bird, being approached, abruptly takes flight—and is not less abruptly transformed:

> And he unrolled his feathers
> And rowed him softer home —
>
> Than Oars divide the Ocean,
> Too silver for a seam —
> Or Butterflies, off Banks of Noon
> Leap, plashless, as they swim.

We should note these differences; at the same time we should not exaggerate or misconstrue them. The one specific critical concern the poet herself proposed to Higginson—are my verses "alive"?—applies to both kinds. The better distinction, then, though necessarily a rough and ready one, may be the distinction between quick drafts—some of them, to be sure, of extraordinary deftness and finish—and completed poems (so far as poems ever are "completed"); poems, that is, that (as we may imagine the poet herself chancing to discover in writing them) were not meant for the next morning, or for the evening's reflection on the afternoon's event, but in some manner for eternity.

Further, and still in the realm of ascertainable fact, we may keep in mind the actual public life of these poems once they began to be made public in any substantial number. It is a fact that the first published collection of the poems, in 1890, went through sixteen printings before the decade was out and continued to be reprinted right up to the moment when better editions became available; this is quite apart from the quick recognition their distinctively poetic qualities won from readers like William Dean Howells and the formidable Alice James as being the thing itself and not some rude or clumsy approximation. Such, we recall, was not the case with the poems of Dickinson's younger contemporary Gerard Manley Hopkins, whose work, also posthumously published, would never reach the same kind of wide public audience.

One of the best critical statements about Emily Dickinson's poetry in the perspective I am raising was one of the very first. It is the response, in a letter to Higginson, of Samuel Gray Ward, a Boston banker who was himself a relic of the high Transcendentalist era; half a century earlier Ward had been at Harvard College with Jones Very and Ellery Channing and had placed essays in *The Dial* and in Elizabeth Peabody's *Aesthetic Papers*. Higginson was, I think, right on target in describing it to Mabel Todd (with whom he had edited the first printing of the poems) as "the most remarkable criticism yet made on Emily Dickinson." It is still not far from that. Samuel G. Ward to Thomas Wentworth Higginson, October 11, 1891:

> My dear Mr. Higginson,
>   I am, with all the world, intensely interested in Emily Dickinson. No wonder six editions have been sold, every copy, I should think, to a New Englander. She may become world famous, or she may never get out of New England. She is the quintessence of that element we all have who are of the Puritan descent *pur sang*. We came to this country to think our own thoughts with nobody to hinder. Ascetics of course, & this our Thebaid. We conversed with our own souls till we lost the art of communicating with other people. The typical family grew up strangers to each other, as in this case. It was *awfully* high, but awfully lonesome. Such prodigies of shyness do not exist elsewhere. We get it from the English, but the

English were not alone in a corner of the world for a hundred & fifty years with no outside interest.

I doubt that scholarship can make too much, in assessing nineteenth-century American writing, of the historical realities here defined. Something comparable to what Coleridge said of the English nation in his time—that for more than two hundred years (since the fratricidal conflicts set off by the English Reformation) it had undergone an arduous and passionate preparation for contemplating and debating the loftiest imaginative ideas—applies *a fortiori* to the population of New England, where the "good old [spiritual] cause" had been, in effect, historically unopposed and had left its mark on every aspect of cultural *praxis*. The consequence, in imaginative terms, was that two centuries after the original settlement this population was constitutionally habituated to speaking of its own life symbolically and even (in the fullest Kierkegaardian sense) ironically. It possessed, it was bred to, an instinctive awareness of the immense disparity between what its life amounted to on an everyday basis and what that life was alleged to be both in the eye of Providence and in the perspectives of devotional self-scrutiny. Or, to borrow the great phrase from Emily Dickinson's own corrective reminder to Higginson about what might be going on inside her poems' personalized idiom, it too—this New England population that Samuel Ward saw as her proper original audience—was prompted by every birthright instinct to conceive of itself and to project itself in discourse as an assemblage of "supposed persons" whose most serious utterances were always something more than the spilling out of private feeling. As indeed will be the case for any human community when in its shared apprehension of life it becomes something more than a numberable crowd of bodies, and lives by what Dickinson's equally extraordinary younger contemporary, Charles Sanders Peirce, would define as its unspoken "interpretant."

This ideal New England community was thoroughly accustomed—to the dangerous point, by the 1840s, of being thoroughly inured—to a vocabulary of grand imaginative abstractions on the ultimate issues of life and death, happiness and grief, contentment or annihilation. It had once positively expected to be addressed in startling and paradoxical language, associative puns and argumentative conundrums. Also it would not have been at all surprised to be told that it would have to "labor" (Blackmur's word) for its imaginative rewards. Indeed the quotient of critical labor Blackmur speaks of as being required of the reader of Emily Dickinson's poems does not seem vastly different from what was expected of the audience for one of Jonathan

Edwards's sermons, or for any evangelical sermon (within the old Congre-
gational order) in which the thoughtful listener is repeatedly challenged to
distinguish between what is true and what falls short of truth, between
witness that is truly inspired and witness that is routinized if not actually
from the devil. Admittedly such austerities of critical and spiritual attention
were largely in retreat during the middle nineteenth century, in New
England as elsewhere. Much of Emily Dickinson's own uneasiness with the
devotional pieties of even those closest and dearest to her came, as her early
letters show, from an intuitive awareness that the received language of faith
had somehow lost contact with the actualities of spiritual perception and
understanding. The old ways of speaking were undergoing, as she came of
age, a massive and irreversible attenuation. But the words themselves
remained erratically in use—more or less the point, we recall, of Dr.
Holmes's witty allegory of the one-hoss shay.

In any event the traditional language of her province—its vocabulary of
high-powered abstractions on ultimate themes along with the well-established habit of surrounding and combining such abstractions with the
sharpest popular or vernacular idiom—was second nature to Emily Dickinson. It takes no special discernment to see that, starting with banner words
like *immortality*, *eternity*, *ordinance*, *grace*, *sacrament*, and the rest, this
vocabulary was an immediate and powerful resource for her poetry. But it
was also a danger to any finer, more exact expressiveness. It was, if anything,
too readily available to her. Richard Wilbur, approaching her with a poet's
consciousness of both practical incentives and practical obstacles, has put
the matter most succinctly in remarking that she inherited "a great and
overbearing vocabulary which, had she used it submissively, would have
forced her to express an established theology and psychology. But she would
not let that vocabulary write her poems for her." And at her steady best—
also, for that matter, at her unsteady best—this seems to me true. She was
not dominated by her vocabulary, her provincial and historical inheritance
of specifying language. Repeatedly, a sharpness of fresh definition comes
into the poems, and it comes by way of juxtaposing the great freighted
liturgical words and word-clusters to the wayward private experience, and
consciousness, attending any persistent use of them. And, to repeat, the
expressive strategies in question would not have been unfamiliar to her
conceivable hearers. So in a well-designed sermon the preacher begins with
a grand word or text and then proceeds (as who should say) to deconstruct
it. But the deconstruction was in this case for an ideally self-supposing
audience that would not only know, or know that it ought to know, the

truest meanings of such words but would also know its own capacity for deconstructive inattention and its regular need for this kind of homeopathic verbal shock-treatment.

The sum of what Emily Dickinson and this presumptive contemporary audience would have shared was of course the imaginative apprehension of life at the heart of the old Puritanism, an apprehension naturally conveyed in metaphors of life as a perpetual state of probation, one's course of life as an embattled pilgrimage, every momentous relationship as, potentially, the sealing of a sacred covenant, and the rest. When she begins a poem, "Our journey had advanced—," I doubt that anyone expected to be listening would have thought it necessary to ask, "What journey?" Nor would any such reader have been greatly surprised by the imagery of dubious battle and apocalyptic resolution overtaking the poem at its end:

> Retreat — was out of Hope —
> Behind — a Sealed Route —
> Eternity's White Flag — Before —
> And God — at every Gate —

The rich, extravagant, Scripture-based idiom of the Protestant hymnal, not less than the habit of vigorous and unnerving preaching, was, as we know, another main resource for her. But this, too, she used in her own fashion. As we may think of a sizeable number of her poems as minisermons, mock sermons, or, frequently, antisermons (consider that excellent Sunday School lesson for her nephew that begins, "The Bible is an antique volume— / Written by faded Men"), so we may read others as antihymns. Or, in a few unforgettable instances, as real hymns though private, in an intenser version of the quietist manner of William Cowper or of Whittier; so, alongside the long-proven popularity of Cowper's "O for a closer walk with God" or Whittier's "Dear Lord and Father of mankind," we may place her even quieter yet more directly piercing voice, "I live with Him — I see His face / I go no more away. . . ."

No, she was not dominated by these genetic resources any more than she was dominated by the transmitted weight of that total historical New England which not only gave shape and substance to her imaginative life but provided, I would further argue, secret assurance that her own voice would not, ever, go absolutely unheard—and this even if she had no other auditor than that most austere of Supposed Persons, at once infinitely remote and oppressively near, whom latter-day New Englanders like the

Dickinsons stubbornly continued praying to though every available sign worked to convince them that He was, at least for the present, in eclipse. ("They are religious—except me—and address an Eclipse every morning— whom they call their 'Father.' ") She was not dominated. She was impressively indomitable, not only in the mid-1850s letter distancing herself for once and for all from her prospective sister-in-law's churchbound faith and prophesying her own acceptance by "a darker spirit," but equally—without fear of retribution—in the efficient comfort of her deathbed note to the Norcrosses: "Little Cousins, Called back." The scholarly business of creating for her one or another fugitive *persona* out of nineteenth-century sentimental romance (or twentieth-century psychoanalytic impertinence) has been notoriously overdone, though of course she herself initiated the practice. A good deal of the time she does present herself, in her letters, in the role of the clever, slyly subversive eighteen-year-old at church—not so much irreverent as reverent at the wrong, the awkward, the inconvenient moment, and with the wrong responses. Or call her, by self-appointment, an "idiot in the family" (as in our time Sartre characterized Flaubert): one who makes it her vocation to say "yes—but!" and whose first piercing wisdom includes detecting, and deflecting, all the subtly projected symptoms in the community around her of terminal self-satisfaction.

But the idiot in the family is also likely to be the one most worth educating. What is more, the family and its nearest friends and well-wishers as often as not know this, obscurely, and know it whether the child in question is a son or a daughter. He or she—she in this case—will be perceived as most worth educating if only because nobody can think of anything else to do with her; most worth encouraging, or putting up with, whatever peculiar course she follows. Edward Dickinson may well have begged his older daughter not to read the books he bought her, but he did after all buy them. And I think it may help to refine our own notions about the older New England and North American society and the place of gifted young women within it (in the restless generation of the 1840s and 1850s, at least) if we consider the possibility that within her nearest community Emily Dickinson's extraordinary gifts were, after a fashion, acknowledged and encouraged, even if on the whole (especially by our careerist standards) rather blindly and within radical limits.

On this conjectural point I can offer one frail bit of supporting evidence from my own odd budget of family recollection and legend. This is through the coincidence that my northern Vermont grandfather had a gifted and, within the family, much mythologized older sister who, born in 1836, was only half a dozen years younger than Emily Dickinson and who—before an early death from tuberculosis at nineteen—was the one child in the family (four sons and a daughter) to be sent beyond the village schools to the advanced collegiate academy at Fort Edward in upper New York State. There she was—allowed? encouraged?—entitled, at any rate, to study French, algebra, history, chemistry, geology, and rhetoric, besides now and again attending lively meetings of the local Young America Society. Gifts of mind and spirit were still respected for their own sake in upcountry New England in those days (as appears less true within the thickening careerism, during the second half of the century, of urbanized centers like Cambridge, Massachusetts, where Alice James's lot was unfortunately cast, another lone sister in a household of boys). Gifts, talents, venturesome opinions were respected even when they took odd or inconvenient form—such disaffection from the respectable new professional-class Whiggery, for example, as may be imputed to a member, c. 1850, of the Young America Society—and, most important, whether they chose a male or a female habitation.[2] Further, they continued to be respected as their bearer advanced into maturity and middle age. So it is always worth recalling (and Richard Sewall's admirably designed biography helps greatly to do so) that besides being the older daughter of a Congressman of the United States and first citizen of his town, Emily Dickinson was at one time or another, including all her years of withdrawal, in regular and prized correspondence with, among others, the editor-in-chief of the *Springfield Republican*, then a newspaper of national influence; with the editor of *Scribner's Monthly*; with another eminent man of letters and public affairs, Colonel Higginson, who had financed John Brown, organized one of the first black regiments in the Civil War, and contributed throughout his life to the *Atlantic Monthly*; with the second leading metropolitan Protestant clergyman in the United States (and Dickinson's preference for Charles Wadsworth over Henry Ward Beecher, Commencement orator at Amherst College in 1862, is distinctly to her credit); with numerous other professional men and women, including young men who fought through the Civil War; and also, not least notably, with the chief judicial officer of the Commonwealth of Massachusetts, who is believed

2. For women, gender prejudice certainly constrained the free expression of such gifts, but the forceful commentary on this hardly secret truth latterly advanced by explicitly feminist criticism is at fault, I think, in commonly failing to recognize the countervailing support and reassurance given—to those capable of exploiting it—by class position, social standing, and family security and pride.

to have proposed to her sometime after her father's death, when she was in her mid-forties.

It constitutes, all in all, a very different community of personal exchange from the one Henry Thoreau frequented in Concord or Herman Melville in New York City, and the difference is not in the direction of ignorance and isolation. And here, we may say, is Emily Dickinson's unassembled audience. More precisely, here is the living shadow and remnant of it, the imagined and implied community of exchange addressed in her poems, that no degree of solitude or incomprehension could wholly deprive her of. As an actual audience it did not, as we know, come together in her lifetime. Toward the end of her life, it was, as even a possible audience, harder to maintain belief in than was the case when her verse style first coalesced. In some sense she herself had to reinvent it each time she spoke out, in poems and letters alike (letters that as time passed fell more and more into the figurative and metrical phrasing of her poems). Essentially it figured to her as an "ungathered" community, or communion, whose members might share at last only a common burden of estrangement, as if always and irreversibly "bound to opposing lands":

> And so when all the time had leaked,
> Without external sound
> Each bound the Other's Crucifix—
> We gave no other Bond—

My claim is simply that it nevertheless remains the community of attention instinctively assumed by the voice, the voices, Dickinson habitually speaks in. And what I have mainly wished to suggest about it is that it was a community which—in her own consciousness of the possibility of it—would not have been unequipped to see what the matter was that she had chosen, each time, to speak about.

What in reality remained of this shadow audience after 1860 would doubtless have found the actual progression of many poems (as Higginson commonly did find them) puzzling, or disturbing, or both. It might still have uneasily sensed rather more of her genuine and shocking originality of spirit than did most of the readers who, a long generation after, began buying her and reading her and who mainly found her (or what was then available of her) charming; but it would almost certainly have underrated her architectonic and expressive inventiveness, or what R. P. Blackmur summed up as "the degree or amount of experience actualized [i.e., poetically] in her verse." That is, it would not as regularly have heard—as those few who had the chance in her lifetime apparently did not, with odd exceptions like the excellent Helen Hunt Jackson, who both heard and memorably told her so—a distinction of statement that was specifically poetic as well as affective and moral. The official community of middle and late nineteenth-century literacy in North America, as represented in the magazinish taste of the time, was a body of persons that in affairs of the spirit seems to us increasingly closed off, in explicit awareness, from its own imaginative inheritance. It was a belletristic community increasingly embarrassed by its forebears' energetic idiom of reflection and self-interrogation, or whatever of this survived, and increasingly fearful of confronting and honestly articulating a whole range of feelings concerning its essential life and prospects. As we know, those who did first read Emily Dickinson's poems in any quantity—Higginson, Mabel Loomis Todd—and who took on the task of presenting her to a public had a good deal of trouble understanding why she had used this or that turn of phrase, prosodic dissonance, or shift and reversal of tone. They felt free to correct the formal indecorousness, as it seemed to them, of her idiosyncratic diction and slant rhymes. But they seem finally not to have doubted her high seriousness, her force in argument, her imaginative vividness, and they did—with conspicuously less hesitation and delay than the legatees of Hopkins's genius—set about getting her into print.

In our own unnerved and unnerving time we can hear her well enough, I suspect. It may even be that we can hear her better, less obstructedly, than Blackmur did in the 1930s with his Eliot-derived prejudice in favor of a fully "objectified" or "depersonalized" workmanship. With the help of American poets who have come of age since 1945—and with the help of Emily Dickinson herself, insofar as most of these newer poets, I would wager, absorbed quite a lot of her from the ambitious national-heritage textbooks and Untermeyeresque anthologies that came into use in American high schools during the 1930s and 1940s—we have, since Blackmur wrote his challenging essay, profitably loosened and pluralized our sense of what can be authentically poetic. We have loosened it enough, I think, to make of his not at all inaccurate phrase for a large part of her work—"a kind of *vers de société* of the soul"—not the term of diminution he meant it to be but (the mode in question being strongly enforced) a term of discriminating praise. Might we not see, for example, the wonderfully mixed personal idiom of John Berryman's *Dream Songs*, one of the genuine verse-inventions of our era, as one latter-day analogue, perhaps descendant, of Dickinson's insistently self-creating voice and compositional freedom?

But my simple general point, in the commonplaces I have been lining out, is that Emily Dickinson's is a poetry we do have to work to continue hearing. Hearing, that is, in its full power of truthfulness and communicative reinforcement. We have to work at staying open to it, as to anything we prize; and for this, nothing is more important than continually returning to it—no one yet knows all its secrets—and exchanging our findings, the pleasure and the provocation alike that we have in it; thus keeping ourselves together as a community of readers and, so to speak, textual friends. By foregathering in an occasion like this to celebrate both the life and the writings, do we not briefly re-create an appropriate community in which the work of the poet and the collaborative work of her readers may find continuance?

4

Adventures of the Young Man

Brockden Brown's Arthur Mervyn

[In the late 1940s, going about graduate school chores, I read a run of novels by an obscure post-Revolutionary Philadelphian, Charles Brockden Brown (1771–1810), and giddily decided that I had uncovered an American Balzac, a novelist whose purposeful originality the canon-makers had somehow not yet properly recognized. Eventually I had to concede that Brown was a good deal less than that, though still of period interest; that as an author he was essentially the sort of individual accident who fills up the margins of specifically literary history, leaving behind no consequential voiceprint yet serving to recall some part of a past era's distinguishing preoccupations, literary or otherwise.

Subsequently, however, and rather to my surprise, a sizeable body of academic commentary began to gather around Brown's four best-known novels (without, I think, his ceasing to be as "obscure and shadowy" as he had been to Hawthorne in the 1840s, who in "The Hall of Fantasy" relegated Brown to a remote corner

in a showroom where the high honors went to Fielding, Richardson, and Scott).
In the new Columbia Literary History of the United States *(1988),* Brown
gets more space than either Dreiser or Edith Wharton; feminist revisionism has
made much of his self-reliant women characters and their psychosocial traumas;
and John Limon's brilliant presentation of Brown's fiction as adumbrating the
long challenge of modern science to every form of literary practice (The Place of
Fiction in the Time of Science: 1990) *makes the strongest case yet for his*
historical significance. The admirable Library of America project has taken him
on, in the wake of an M.L.A.-sponsored "collected" edition. Yet the full-length
accounts of Brown's imaginative career now on library shelves, like Norman
Grabo's The Coincidental Art of Charles Brockden Brown *(1981), do seem*
to me to have invented a figure more autonomous and coherent than the texts
warrant. The most stylish and original of these, Marisa Bulgheroni's La Tenta-
zione della Chimera *(1963), effectively re-creates an author out of the Euro-*
pean Sturm und Drang, an author who very well ought to have existed whether
or not he actually did.

At intervals these later testimonies have tempted me to update my own early
arguments for Brown's angular merit. But I think it better all around to leave the
following account as it originally appeared, in 1957, making only a few incidental
corrections and abridgments.]

Though the novels of Charles Brockden Brown were never widely popular,
they held the attention of a surprising number of Brown's juniors and betters
(Shelley and Poe, W. H. Prescott and Margaret Fuller, who labeled him "a
novelist by far our first in point of genius and instruction as to the soul of
things"), and because they did, it isn't possible to remain content with the
usual evaluation of Brown's achievement. Shelley's extravagant admiration,
recorded in Peacock's memoir, is the notorious instance, but even the
Edinburgh Review, two decades after his death, looked back on Brown as "a
man of genius," one of a handful of American writers worthy of commendation not merely as transatlantic curiosities but on their own merit. If
Brown were, as frequently described, only a purveyor of the conventions of
Gothic romance, such a verdict would be hard to understand; by the first
third of the nineteenth century these conventions had become matters of
parody and ridicule. It would be foolish to claim too much for his novels;
the narrative technique *is* crude, the style cumbersome, the execution often
careless and erratic. Allowances must be made, and it is understandable that
as much attention has been paid to the circumstances of Brown's career as
possibly our "first professional man of letters" as to the quality and scope of

his work in fiction. But if he is to be kept in view, for whatever purpose, it is the second matter that should concern us.

By the end of this essay readers may have assented in general to the analysis offered here and yet feel that much that should be of central concern has been left untouched: questions of the provenance of Brown's intellectual habit and energy (what difference did it make that he came of Quaker stock? that his early training was in the law?), of the implicit critique in his work of the assumptions of eighteenth-century rationalism, of the symbolic judgment put upon American society and American destiny in the anxious early years of the republic. My hope is that a way into these broader questions may be suggested by what follows. Certainly some preliminary assessment of the work itself is required: what are the actual, encountered qualities of Brown's fiction? On what might the *Edinburgh* reviewer's opinion have been based? My starting point is simply the fact that three of Brown's novels pursue a single theme, that of the young man's initiation into the world's life. This is, however, one of the classic themes of the novel since the time of *Tom Jones* and *The Sorrows of Young Werther*; and my assumption is that to examine in detail Brown's treatment of this theme may furnish a better notion of his interest as a writer than do the sensationalist terrors of *Wieland* or the Gothic psychology of *Ormond*, for which he is usually remembered.

Of these three novels, all written between 1798 and 1800, *Edgar Huntly* is still close to Gothic allegory. Form and matter alike are schematic and dreamlike; and though Brown adapts Gothic convention to a serious rendering of certain problematic moral and psychological states, as well as making a point in his preface about the story's specifically American setting, the central action is self-engendering and dissociated, dealing with the kind of experience Henry James attributed to *romance*—"experience disengaged, disembroiled, disencumbered, exempt from the conditions that we usually know to attach to it." But in the unfinished *Stephen Calvert* and most strikingly in *Arthur Mervyn*, the basic moral action is less disengaged, less exempted. The "world" the young man enters is given a more substantial and independent specification. The result is an increase in range and narrative energy that carries Brown's fiction outward from the psychological *récit*, the case study, toward the variety and scope of the full-dress novel. *Edgar Huntly* is subtitled "Memoirs of a Sleep-Walker," and as with ventriloquism and insanity in *Wieland* Brown takes an informed clinical interest in the phenomenon of somnambulism. But in *Arthur Mervyn* a further dimension of experience is taken in; the subtitle is now "Memoirs of the Year

1793." With a minor writer much of the interest of such an enlargement of focus is in its potential major; perhaps it is not out of place to recall that Stendhal, setting his first proper novel in the same tradition of the young man's education, was to define it not as the "Memoirs of Julien Sorel" but as a "Chronicle of the Nineteenth Century."

2

The *Memoirs of Stephen Calvert*, which ran serially in Brown's *Monthly Magazine and American Review* from June 1799 through June 1800, is at once more improbably melodramatic in plot than even *Edgar Huntly* and more realistic in every other respect. The change is potentially for the better. The context of *Calvert* loses a little for being less symbolically suggestive than that of *Huntly* with its caves, wild animals, secret chests, and bloodbaths, but there is a marked gain in the basic commodities of dialogue and characterization. There are even touches of a humor rare in Brown, and no falling off in mystery and suspense. But these achievements in *Calvert* are the by-product of a general failure, of which the most obvious sign is that the novel was left unfinished, abandoned at the first big plot climax. Brown, who normally pushed his narratives through in a single flourish or not at all, apparently could not get hold of a manageable story in the situation he had devised. The plot, of twin brothers separated at birth and pursuing opposite destinies toward reunion, suggests what went wrong; a novelist of developed talent might turn so crude a device to account (as Wilkie Collins would do in *Armadale*), but it was not salvageable by Brown's primitive craft.

Yet purely as a device it is not more absurd than the sleepwalking of *Edgar Huntly* or the ventriloquism of *Wieland*. It raises equal possibilities for representing ambiguities of conduct and consciousness, as the synthetic mystifications of the *doppelgänger* convention could support for Poe the precise fable of "William Wilson." There is much in *Calvert* to indicate some such intention. So Stephen, driven to the wall by the mystery of his "other self," exclaims: "The wisest and soberest of human beings is, in some respects, a madman; that is, he acts against his better reason, and his feet stand still, or go south, when every motive is busily impelling him north." Every *known* motive: another character is driven to the baffled admission that to explain human conduct one must assume the operation of secret causes, motives inscrutable to human reason: "The world is eternally producing what to our precipitate judgment, are prodigies, anomalies, monsters. Innate, dastardly, sordid wickedness frequently springs up where genial temperature and wise culture have promised us the most heavenly products." Such reflections, editorial but not uninteresting, could be made vividly impressive in a novel if they were dramatized by the story, substantiated by its predicaments. But in *Calvert* Brown did not bring off this concurrence of action and idea. The mysteries that are to be explained by the lost brother, the moral tension that marks the best of Brown's fiction, are dissipated by the crudeness of the explanation itself.

What remains is the sketch of a romantic egoist, whose initiation into the world is defined by his experience of love. Love is presented in three modes: as a psychologically ambiguous passion, as a settled social convention, and as a moral anomaly. There was rich ground for conflict and tension here, which the cult of *Werther* had not exhausted. In Benjamin Constant's *Adolphe*, a decade later, the analysis of youthful sensibility caught up in the toils of love is carried through with dialectical subtlety and psychological precision. But the comparison emphasizes the narrow margin of Brown's talent: his fiction may be called psychological, but its psychology tends to be abstract and mechanistic. He could approach that dialectic of moral consequences which, in Constant's novel, is the substructure of the play of feeling, but he could not flesh it out into sustained dramatic relationships. As it is, he comes remarkably close to succeeding. The social world of *Calvert* is sharply and engagingly drawn; the women are particularly convincing;[1] there is an observant and persuasive realism in rendering the electric atmosphere of city life. The setting, in short, is potentially adequate to Stephen's responses, and ampler in fact than that of *Adolphe*. But Brown does not make it integral to Stephen's experience, which stems instead from the factitious circumstance of the lost brother. As a result, the ideas projected in the novel are still-born.

They are, however, worth examining, for they recur in the much superior *Arthur Mervyn* as determining assumptions. Love, "a motley and complex sentiment . . . the growth, not of reason, but of sense," figures in Brown's scheme as the great enemy of reason; it compounds selfishness with irrationality, and delivers men over to hypocrisy, jealousy, and chronic dissimula-

---

1. Several early nineteenth-century critics, notably Edward Tyrrel Channing in the *North American Review*, were captivated by the women in *Calvert*, especially by the portrait of Stephen's cousin Louisa, a very plain, ordinary, unromanticized young woman. Both Louisa and Clelia Neville express themselves with such unembarrassed candor and energy that we are led to suspect a deliberate counter-statement to the sentimentalist version of female character.

tion (here Brown's insights are positively Proustian). "Misguided passions," it is argued, "make many a man a paradox," leading either to imposture or blind self-deception. So Stephen, in love, is overwhelmed by the impulses and "quick transitions" of passion and its forced commitments. In all his turnings there is the hint of a shrinking from his sexual nature, a tendency he shares with several of Brown's protagonists—Shelley's beloved Constantia Dudley of *Ormond*, for example—as of course with no small fraternity of Romantic heroes. Certainly his experience is more or less directly identified with sexuality. But if the identification were more insistent, it would be less effective; the psychological phenomena Brown works with remain serviceable, as he often forgets, insofar as a merely clinical explanation is avoided.

For the moral conflict revolves not around sexuality but around the more abstract concept of "energy." Passion is dangerous not because it arouses sexual drives (which, after all, both society and literary convention know how to channel) but because it releases this more general dynamism in human nature. What may be taken in *Calvert* as a thematic sentence neatly underscores the double nature of "energy," a force at the heart of Romantic psychology: "There is an energy in the human mind which enables it to conquer every inquietude, or a flexibility that reconciles itself to every restraint." To enter the world one must possess energy—the creatural force, the *vis renovans*, in the central being of man. But its perverse counterpart is "flexibility," "versatility," energy thwarted and turned in on itself. Its first instinct is to master experience, but its second is to possess without responsibility; it covets the path of least resistance. As a young man, a creature of energy, Stephen is ambitious to develop but comes to discover the moral blindness of his ambition. His self-absorption is self-consuming; he is defeated less by the "world" than by himself. And though in the end he seeks release by escaping to solitude and penitential labor in the western wilderness, even this, Brown's narrative implies, will not save him, so deeply is he compromised, so far weakened.

Which is to say that though the execution fell short, there were rich possibilities in *Stephen Calvert*, and it is a pity that Brown failed to realize them.

3

Arthur Mervyn, however, is another story. In the first place it is unique among Brown's four main novels: it ends happily. Otherwise the design is not, superficially, very different. There are the same elements that Brown called for in various prefaces: "trials of fortitude and constancy," illustrations of the "moral constitution of man," the display of "soaring passions and intellectual energy." It is in fact his fullest treatment of the fable of initiation. Especially in comparison with the near-allegory of *Edgar Huntly*, the external world into which the hero advances on his quest for experience seems spacious and substantial; and the novel as a whole seems the least claustral of Brown's work, the most natural in incident and motive, as it is his most moderate and plausible treatment of his hero's inward development. Arthur Mervyn discharges his energies, but quite within his original frame of character; there is here no overwhelming "transformation" (the subtitle of *Wieland*). Arthur survives unharmed and little changed. Instead of anguish and ordeal, there is the steady progress of a "fearless and sedate manner," an "unalterable equanimity," through every danger and error. In *Arthur Mervyn* Brown's dark fables of transformation give way to a comedy of success.

That is not to say that this is a comic novel or that Brown has changed the world of his fiction into a place of happiness and good will. *Arthur Mervyn* is comedy only in the most general sense—with regard to a choice of tone that rejects opportunities to judge life as tragic or damned, and to a plot in which not even the most shocking events are given any especially horrific coloring. Among Brown's principal novels it is the one most free of Gothic sensationalism. It is a bitter comedy, set in a cruel and poisonous city world—a setting defined by the inhumanities of commercial society and by an even more dehumanizing visitation of epidemic pestilence, these being the outward trials the hero must pass through. But uniquely in Brown's fiction the hero of *Arthur Mervyn* survives them unscathed; they only spur his successful advance. The world has not changed for the better in Brown's imagination, but here he has invented a hero who instinctively discovers what can be done with it and in it.[2]

In *Stephen Calvert* what is done in the end is to flee to the primeval wilderness. There is no wilderness in *Arthur Mervyn* to oppose to the city; the contrast is rather with an unpolluted countryside of farms and freemen, the Jeffersonian hinterland. Brown draws directly on the moral sociology of

2. *Arthur Mervyn* may be compared to Royall Tyler's *The Algerine Captive* (1797), also about the initiation of a young provincial into a wider world. Tyler's novel is comedy of a brittler sort, its plot a mere convenience for the satiric purpose. It is still readable, with a worldly (though heavy-handed) gaiety quite foreign to Brown's somber manner, but with nothing of the moral tension generated in Brown's fiction.

eighteenth-century agrarianism; Arthur's first adventures set the corrupt city
against an idyll of "cornfield and threshing floor," stock-market sharping
against honest rural labor. He has no money, no trade, no liberal education,
and admits that his experience is "slender." In his natural desire to make a
place for himself he is drawn to the city. But insofar as that desire is
balanced by the desire for independence and untrammeled happiness, he
cannot "outroot from his mind the persuasion that to plough, to sow, and
to reap, were employments most befitting a reasonable creature, and from
which the truest pleasure and the least pollution would flow." Only "the
trade of ploughman was friendly to health, liberty, and pleasure." Nevertheless, given immediate motive by a quarrel with his father and the loss of his
patrimony, he sets off for Philadelphia, feeling that at last he is "mounted
into man."

In a few hours the city's merciless custom has overthrown all his prospects.
Like Karl Rossman in Kafka's *Amerika*, he has been cheated of his last
pocket change, his bundle has been stolen, and the practical joke of a
speciously benevolent young man-about-town has left him trapped inside a
strange house in the circumstance of a thief, so that he must leave behind
his only pair of shoes in order to escape (the theme is betrayal, but the
manner is very close to a burlesque on the Gothic melodrama of dark houses
and secret closets). Destitution throws him on the mercy of the merchant
Welbeck, soon discovered to be a forger and murderer, a confidence man of
dangerous energy, and before Arthur's involvement with Welbeck has
ended, he has been implicated in Welbeck's crimes; the city has branded
him not with the name and fortune he has come to seek but with
commercial dishonor, its own worst colors.

The yellow-fever epidemic only confirms the image Arthur has formed of
the city as a place of "confusion and panic." The terrors of the plague,
Brown specifies, "exterminated all the sentiments of nature": "Wives were
deserted by husbands, and children by parents. Some had shut themselves
in their houses, and debarred themselves from all communication with the
rest of mankind." The plague defines the city for us: a place of contagion
where all decencies are corrupted and men perish "in the public ways,"
sickened by the atmosphere and abandoned by their own families. Through
all these misadventures Arthur remembers his refuge: "The country was my
sole asylum." At the height of the plague the whole city is in flight to open
country; Arthur, caught up in the rout, senses that the "floating pestilence"
ends at the bridge which is the gate to the city and, crossing, puts his trust
"in the pure air of the country."

But Arthur Mervyn is no conventional pastoralist. Brown's image of the commercial city was formed not from rural prejudice but from abundant inside knowledge (his father and brothers were Philadelphia merchants, and he spent his life in Philadelphia and New York). His moral image of the country was equally critical. The "fortitude and independence" of rural manners, Arthur admits, are a mixed blessing. In a farm household there may be "fonder and more rational attachments of friendship" than the cash relations of the metropolis will allow, and that is good; Arthur's country life with the Quaker Hadwins becomes an interlude of affection and sincerity. But his own rural family is as brutish as it is robust, as spiritually degraded as it is physically independent. No pastoral scruple keeps him from loathing his yeoman father. Agricultural labors, he reflects, may produce health and beauty, but they rob man of his best capacities as man: "What was to be dreaded from them was their tendency to quench the spirit of liberal curiosity." He cannot reverse the revolution in his mind that the city has effected. In five days he has gathered there "more instruction than from the whole tissue of [his] previous existence." His new education has fitted him for "activity and change"; it has been an "apprenticeship to fortitude and wisdom," and he now asserts that "if cities are the chosen seats of misery and vice, they are likewise the soil of all the laudable and strenuous productions of mind."

Precisely as in the end he rejects the agrarian stereotype, Brown's image of the city is more persuasive than the political caricature of the agrarians. It is no less a nightmare city, and the nightmare is spelled out in dreadful detail. But it is not the cause of evil, merely the place of it; it is the setting that, for Brown, best represents the moral chaos in the social behavior of man. In good times this disturbing moral reality is perhaps out of sight, as in *Arthur Mervyn* the financial scheming, the sordid subplots, are at first out of sight; the plague uncovers it with shocking violence, but so, the narrative shows, may any daily encounter. It is, in short, the probable law of nature and the certain truth about human society.

The most striking images for Brown's nightmare metropolis are rendered through Arthur's emergent consciousness, his response to the novelties of his situation. As he walks through the pestilence-ridden city, what he notices first is its "dreary solitude," the exact reverse of its usual confident bustle:

> Between the verge of the Schuylkill and the heart of the city I met
> not more than a dozen figures; and these were ghost-like, wrapped in

cloaks, from behind which they cast me glances of wonder and suspicion, and, as I approached, changed their course, to avoid touching me. Their clothes were sprinkled with vinegar, and their nostrils defended from contagion by some powerful perfume.

It is the quiet of death, broken only by the profanity of the hearse-drivers. The self-sufficiency Arthur seeks is perversely realized; he is "surrounded by the habitations of men," but no doors will open to him, and he reflects: "Never, in the depths of caverns or forests, was I equally conscious of loneliness." In all his novels Brown worked at placing the action in suitably provocative or symbolic settings, like the cave and wilderness of *Edgar Huntly*. Too often his effects seem manufactured. The notable achievement in *Arthur Mervyn* is his occasional skill at rendering his whole ominous image of existence in brief descriptive passages that are cut down to a literal clarity of observation, firmly tied to the plot, but alive to his whole conception. Perhaps the finest occurs as Arthur starts across the Delaware, in flight, and gazes back at the city:

> I cast my eyes occasionally at the scene which I had left. Its novelty, joined with the incidents of my condition, threw me into a state of suspense and wonder which frequently slackened my hand and left the vessel to be driven by the downward current. Lights were sparingly seen, and these were perpetually fluctuating, as masts, yards, and hulls were interposed, and passed before them. In proportion as we receded from the shore, the clamors seemed to multiply, and the suggestion that the city was involved in confusion and uproar did not easily give way to maturer thoughts. *Twelve* was the hour cried, and this ascended at once from all quarters, and was mingled with the baying of dogs, so as to produce trepidation and alarm.

If Brown's reputation among his early admirers has proved puzzling to us, it may be because we have overlooked the force and accuracy of perception, and the simple constructive power, without which such a passage could not have been written.

4

The effect in *Arthur Mervyn* of natural realism and a significant clarity and density of scene is a measure of Brown's success in matching theme and narrative detail. By comparison with his other novels, full of labored soliloquies, there is a corresponding simplification in the handling of his hero. Like all Brown's protagonists Arthur is acutely self-conscious, scrutinizing all his feelings and motives, but only in the later stages of the second volume does the characterization come to depend on lengthy self-analysis. Arthur is represented rather by what he does, what happens to him; he is not so much characterized as brought to life, thrust into action. The lurid setting of the "Memoirs of a Sleep-Walker" is a symbolic projection of Edgar Huntly's half-hidden consciousness. But the setting of the "Memoirs of the Year 1793" exists independently (though not unrelatedly), and the character of Arthur Mervyn is his manner of moving through it; his "maturer thoughts" emerge out of the particular "confusion and uproar" of his city experiences. And where Brown's other narrators stretch their experience into universal propositions about the nature and condition of man, Arthur Mervyn stops short and is content to formulate a prudential rule of conduct. He makes the practical, short-term adjustment; he is not "transformed"; he gets along as he can.

He is, though, all in all, an odd young man; there is a peculiar cast to his successfulness. What Dr. Stevens (the introductory narrator to whom Arthur tells his story) first notices about him is a preternatural gravity. Yellow fever has "decayed" his features, but Stevens sees in them traces of "uncommon but manlike beauty," "pathetic seriousness," and feels a "powerful and sudden claim" laid on his own affections. This magnetic attractiveness is matched by the force of Arthur's curiosity and the imperturbable meddlesomeness of his good will. What Brown presents as curiosity we are more likely to call compulsiveness; behind it stand barely admissible fears. In a literal sense Arthur must escape the malign inheritance that so far has formed his character—not simply ignorance and rusticity but a fatal "defect of constitution" that has killed off his brothers and sisters and holds before him, too, the prospect of early death. Before he has reversed this negative destiny, it threatens to overtake him in the form of the pestilence; paradoxically, what chiefly enables him to survive the deadly effluvia of yellow fever is his calmness, his indifference to danger, his low-pitched willingness to let the pestilence be the death of him if it must.

That false fulfillment he may not accept. If the alternative is death, he must take hold of life at any cost. This is the crux of his education out of moral inertia. The "selfishness" of this necessity requires for compensation just that energy of compassion which he displays in the novel, for the moral cost of his education, in Brown's narrative, is an inbred strain of cruelty and inhumanity. That is the cost for Edgar Huntly and Stephen Calvert, too, who must give injury to others to protect themselves, but for them it is equated with suffering and remorse. In *Arthur Mervyn* it is equated with happiness. For Arthur does not give way in any part of his determination to wind up, as he does, "the happiest of men."

His relationship with Welbeck, the Byronic forger, is central.[3] The very model of energy and experience, a Vautrin to Arthur's Rastignac, Welbeck becomes Arthur's mentor, mocking the common morality of commercial society and living a devious, high-spirited life of crime. Welbeck's wickedness is equivocal, for as one of his business rivals remarks, his extraordinary talents are in good part practiced on fools and usurers who deserve what they get from him. But he is not Schiller's virtuous bandit; he also preys on the honest and poor. And he is no superman; in the end the gray business veterans who are his antagonists counter-trick him, weaving a "tissue of extortions and frauds" that perfectly defines the metropolitan world of 1793. Arthur's first full exposure to this world makes him privy to the plot against Welbeck; taken into Welbeck's service, he conceives it his overriding duty to protect his benefactor. Once Welbeck has become an object for benevolence, Arthur clings to him like a leech. Despite the magnitude of his master's crimes, he remains loyal and forgiving, in defiance of the law and of public opinion. He risks his own fortune in order to save the sinner, is willing to stand accused of partnership in Welbeck's schemes in order to express what he calls his gratitude. All this takes courage and strength of will, to persist in exercising a compassion that has no place in the world's common custom.

But to Welbeck himself Arthur's adhesive benevolence suggests something other than virtuous compassion. "Is there no means of evading your pursuit?" Welbeck cries; "are you actuated by some demon to haunt me, like the ghost of my offences, and cover me with shame?" What he cannot endure is Arthur's righteousness: "What have I to do with that dauntless yet guiltless front? with that foolishly confiding and obsequious, yet erect and unconquerable spirit?" Arthur's concern is unrelenting. He follows Welbeck even to jail and announces that as a first step toward restoring him "to innocence and peace," he has told Dr. Stevens the whole story as he knows it. Welbeck, with everything to hide, is naturally stupefied and accuses Arthur of perfidy—"this outrage upon promises, this violation of faith."

---

3. This is Brown's most obvious borrowing from the precedent of Godwin's *Caleb Williams* (1794), in Caleb's relationship to the dangerous Falkland.

Such energy of goodness is altogether too much for Welbeck, who curses his protégé as an "infernal messenger" and blames him for all their misfortunes since first coming together.

Welbeck is a conscienceless criminal. Yet something in his accusation sticks. Arthur pleads innocence and good intentions, but in the very act of trying to help Welbeck he tips his hand:

> Shall I not visit and endeavor to console thee in thy distress? Let me, at least, ascertain thy condition, and be the instrument in repairing the wrongs which thou hast inflicted. *Let me gain, from the contemplation of thy misery, new motives to sincerity and rectitude.* [Emphasis added.]

His benevolence, we see, is selfish, acquisitive, in no way disinterested. In that respect, of course, it is only human and equips him for the speckled world he must exercise it in. But the ambiguity of his motives will not bother him; conscience untroubled, he ignores Welbeck's accusation and piously shepherds him to his death. Granting that his own behavior has been "ambiguous and hazardous, and perhaps wanting in discretion," he nevertheless pleads that his motives are "unquestionably pure." And he caps this complacent judgment with a balanced and now tested formula for success in the world:

> Good intentions, unaided by knowledge, will, perhaps, produce more injury than benefit, and, therefore, knowledge must be gained, but the acquisition is not momentary; is not bestowed unasked and untoiled for. Meanwhile we must not be inactive because we are ignorant. Our good purposes must hurry to performance, whether our knowledge be greater or less.

Hurrying to performance, Mervyn's good purposes are as catalyzing in their way as Welbeck's concerted malevolence. He is without a sense of privacy, is incapable of embarrassment. He must take charge of everyone's destiny and oversee every private catastrophe with his own eyes. Another's suffering only feeds his appetite for experience. The woman who will complete his march to happiness, Mrs. Fielding, bowled over by his abrupt manners, tells him she has never met with his like, and he confesses: "Ordinary rules were so totally overlooked in my behavior that it seemed impossible for anyone who knew me to adhere to them. No option was left but to admit my claims to friendship and confidence or to reject them altogether." How discomforting his insidious sociability can be, how ruthless his virtue, he seems to have no idea, and he describes the method of his benevolence without understanding what his strong verb may imply: "Every one had my sympathy and kindness, without claiming it, but I *claimed* the kindness and sympathy of every one."

He keeps enough rural ingenuousness, however, to profess astonishment that Mrs. Achsa Fielding, whose kindness and sympathy he takes as his due, should also love him and be eager to marry him. This event, which completes his initiation into the world, gives off the curious overtones characteristic of all his displays of feeling and energy. According to Peacock, it stirred Shelley's enthusiasm for Brown to a rare reservation: "The transfer of the hero's affections from a simple peasant girl to a rich Jewess, displeased Shelley extremely, and he could only account for it on the ground that it was the only way in which Brown could bring his story to an uncomfortable conclusion."[4] Shelley's displeasure expressed an abstract prejudice; the pure young countryman should of course form the pure and not the convenient life-attachment. But the rest of his judgment is oddly penetrating. Why *should* Brown be thought to have wanted to bring his story to an "uncomfortable conclusion"? If Arthur's final happiness is uncomfortable, his own calculations will not admit it. But below his calculations we see that his mind is troubled; the signs are a fit of sleepwalking and a frightful dream in which a voice cries, "Mervyn shall sleep no more!" and he is stabbed by an enraged apparition of the dead Mr. Fielding.

All this is only an interlude before the happy ending; Arthur easily brushes the dream from his mind. But there remains something distasteful about his love. Like his curiosity and his compassion, it has an unsavory air of bare-faced selfishness. He is attracted to Mrs. Fielding because she possesses "that very knowledge in which I was most deficient, and on which I set the most value—the knowledge of the human heart." Such knowledge is indeed power; the lust for it we traditionally think of as not less than satanic. But what has caused Arthur Mervyn a passing uneasiness is not likely to be any qualm on this score. It is rather the suspicion that he may himself be susceptible to love and his own heart exposed, so that his perfect control will be threatened. And in the metropolis of 1793 he would have reason to be uneasy; counterpointing the heartless world of commercial

4. The girl is not a "peasant" except in Shelley's anti-feudal imagination, but the educated daughter of an affluent Quaker gentleman. It is true that Mervyn puts her aside rather casually.

banditry in *Arthur Mervyn* is a wretched succession of misalliances and ill-fated commitments to passion, given to us in a series of secondary episodes too complicated to summarize but serving for all their disconnectedness to reinforce the main themes of the book. But Arthur has prudently forestalled such dangers by making a marriage in which no really new commitment need be made and no new emotion is required of him, accepting as his wife an older woman whom he can fondly call his "mama." In fits of embarrassing complacence he psychoanalyzes himself, recalling proudly how he hated his father but adored a doting mother, and how he easily resisted the advances of his wanton stepmother, being himself "so formed that a creature like her had no power over my senses." So he explains away his feeling for Mrs. Fielding ("Was she not the substitute of my lost mama?") and cheerfully confides this thought to her: "Are you not my lost mama come back again?"

He has made his place in the world, but there has been no real contest; he is, we see now, the world's peculiar match from the start. A chameleon of convenient virtue, able "without design and without effort" to assume the form and role that others wish him to assume, Arthur has the look of a moral sharper of the most invincible sort, a modern bourgeois teenage Tartuffe. Or call him the first full-length portrait in our fiction of a new moral phenomenon: that strange new child-man, the native American. That is, he has fulfilled his nature, but by letting it stay partial, deficient. And I should say that it is this deficiency in the hero—and Brown's apparent indifference to it—that more than any structural or stylistic weakness circumscribes *Arthur Mervyn* and sets it below the great Romantic novels of a young man's education. Welbeck can be Arthur's teacher but not, as Balzac's Vautrin is to Rastignac, his tempter, for Arthur has an untemptable and in that one critical respect an uninteresting character. In the unchallenged fulfillment of his native energies he is unique among Brown's fictional heroes. The essential comedy of his success is that the unwholesome world he moves through (the world projected in most of Brown's fiction) has for the first time been overcome—by a corresponding unwholesomeness of character.

Arthur Mervyn, read in this way, is a cynical book. But the emotions, the operation of mind, back of cynicism, however unconscious, are at least more complex than those that go with mere terror and physical shock. In *Arthur Mervyn* Brown broke out of the mode of psychological melodrama and worked toward a broader and more disturbing image of life. He turned the corner, we may say, from Gothic romance to the more varied prospect of the nineteenth-century novel—a considerable if imperfect achievement.

From another viewpoint we might choose to say that through his steady interest in the perverse irregularities of human conduct he challenged the orderly eighteenth-century classifications of human nature and psychology. (It is worth recalling Brown's informed interest in psychopathic medicine; his closest friend was the Connecticut author and physician Dr. Elihu Hubbard Smith.) From yet another, not unrelated, we might see his work as creating an image of society and human character as they will be found anywhere, even in America the new-found land, that profoundly challenged the new republic's assumptions of progress and civic virtue, its resolute historical optimism. But we could not usefully assert any of these things if the novel were as convention-bound as Brown's fiction is usually made out to be. *Arthur Mervyn* is stamped, however fitfully, with the seriousness and scattershot vitality of Brown's own intelligence, qualities that make his writing, despite all that divides and discourages us from it, well worth returning to.

5

The Scandal of Kate Chopin

The name "Kate Chopin," attached to the work of a Louisiana-based story writer of the 1890s, has the ring of a particularly apt pseudonym. Among the numerous local-color writers of the time, most of them women, pen names were much in fashion. Yet nothing is more symptomatic of Kate Chopin's singular place in American literary history than that this foreign-sounding compound was in fact her proper name. Born Katherine O'Flaherty in St. Louis in 1851, she had begun to write in earnest as the still young widow of Oscar Chopin, a Louisiana merchant and man of property whose ancestry was wholly French. She was herself half French, her mother being of Huguenot and Creole descent and keeping in speech and manner something of the slurred accent and soft formality of the Creole gentry. (Her father had come to America, at eighteen, from Catholic Galway in the 1820s.) Except for a scattering of immigrant sojourners like Crèvecoeur in the late colonial period or Lafcadio Hearn a century later, Kate Chopin is the first consequential figure in American writing whose birthright consciousness and literary taste were formed outside the Protestant, Anglo-Scottish matrix of our older cultural history. We have, really, to look no further for the outward sources of those qualities in her work—the casually secure freedom of mind and feeling, the easy grace of form, the relative indifference to Grundyite prohibitions—that set her apart from the capable run of dialect-writers and local-color realists filling the magazines in her day.

Her family's prominence in mid-nineteenth-century St. Louis (by 1870 the third largest city in the United States) ensured her from early childhood a privileged and abundantly varied experience of life. By contrast, the sectarian villages in New England and the newly settled Middle West, from which so many of her contemporaries emerged, may seem an almost insuperable handicap to imaginative maturity. Her father's death in a train accident in 1855 meant a straitening of family life; yet the household—with her French-speaking grandmother and great-grandmother still living and briskly active—remained the center of a complex network of family ties and interests. A taste for music and belles-lettres was in the expected order of things, with not a trace of high-minded prejudice against romantic fiction. The telling of stories and anecdotes out of the Creole past merged with gossip about present-day intrigues and infidelities; there seems to have been no intrusive sense that young souls should be kept in ignorance of the tangle of adult affairs.

Formal schooling began when she entered, in 1860, the Academy of the Sacred Heart in St. Louis. There, the sense of what was proper for a young lady's education seems to have been as liberal as at home. By her middle teens she was mixing Chateaubriand, Goethe, Mme. de Staël, Lamartine, and Victor Hugo with Bulwer, Lamb, *Lady Blessington's Conversations with Byron*, and Macaulay on Ranke on the Popes (so the contents of a common-place book tell us). The Civil War, in which her family took the Southern side, was a time of special and continuous excitement, and of renewed family sorrow. Her half-brother (by her father's first marriage) was taken prisoner by Union troops in 1862 and, though exchanged a few months later, died of typhoid the next winter; and her beloved great-grandmother Charleville, who had been born in St. Louis at the time of the American Revolution and had lived under both Spanish and French rule, died at eighty-two in 1863.

Finished with school in 1868, Kate O'Flaherty entered promptly upon a strenuous and uninhibited social life. Her diary reports "parties, operas,

concerts, skating and amusements *ad infinitum.*" The interruption of Lent
deflected her only slightly; she could perform at her German Reading Club
and for Holy Thursday plan a round of visits to the city's churches by
moonlight. She read freely, turned over questions of the meaning of things
until she was weary ("reasoning, reasoning, reasoning till night and coming
to no conclusions"), and in her diary wrote down with some satisfaction the
remark of a friend—"a gentleman, of course"—that she "had a way in
conversation of discovering a person's characteristics, opinions, and private
feelings, while they knew no more about me at the end than they knew at
the beginning of the conversation." ("Is this laudable?" she added.) In
March of 1869 she traveled in a family party down the Mississippi to
Louisiana, and found herself immensely attracted to New Orleans, from the
flowers and early strawberries to the charm and civility of social manners.
She met the Louisianan Oscar Chopin in St. Louis the next winter; in his
mid-twenties, he was the son of a wealthy French-born doctor and plantation owner who had emigrated shortly after Waterloo. Soon after her
nineteenth birthday she was engaged to be married. She may well have felt
that it was high time; her mother and the women in her mother's family
back to its American beginnings had been married at fifteen or sixteen.
Childhood in the old Creole households was in no sense artificially sheltered
or prolonged.

Her marriage took place on June 9, 1870, the day beginning with early
Mass among a full gathering of friends and moving forward to a champagne
party on a train bound east for Philadelphia (described in her journal as drab
and Quakerish) and New York ("a great den of swindlers," Oscar decided
after visiting Wall Street). Late in June the young couple sailed for Bremen
and began a honeymoon tour of the Rhineland. Beyond doubt its interest
for them intensified with the sudden outbreak of war between France and
Prussia in mid-July. (At Stuttgart Kate Chopin met Von Moltke "face to
face" on a hotel stairway and got from his "iron countenance" an impression
that the French armies were in for trouble.) Travel plans had to be changed;
the Chopins crossed into Switzerland the last week of July, and were delayed
in getting through to Paris, their principal goal, until the beginning of
September. They traveled knowledgeably and resourcefully, quite at ease in
Europe, with of course no trouble about language once they were in French-
speaking territory, and with a full consciousness of the high drama and
significance of the historical moment. The contrast between the tone of
Kate Chopin's diary and the greenhorn outlook of the famous *Quaker City*
tour of 1867, as recorded in Mark Twain's *Innocents Abroad*, could hardly be

greater. On the 4th of September the Chopins watched from the steps of the Madeleine as crowds streamed by shouting "Vive la République!" "I have seen a French Revolution!" Kate wrote—but admitted a certain sadness at the smashing down of imperial emblems all across the city.

The war curtailed their visit; in a week they were in Brest, bound for home. They began their life together in New Orleans that fall, with Oscar in the gentleman's business of "cotton factor and commission merchant." Their first child was born in May 1871; by the end of the decade there were five sons and a daughter. During the 1870s Kate Chopin made frequent visits back to St. Louis, three of her children being born there; the hot summers were regularly spent at the Creole resort of Grande Isle on the Gulf Coast—the scene of Mme. Lebrun's pension in the story "At Chênière Caminada" and in *The Awakening*. The accumulating burden of financial and agricultural depression after the mid-1870s resulted, however, in the failure of Oscar Chopin's business in 1879, and that winter the young family moved two hundred miles into west-central Louisiana to the village of Cloutierville, twenty miles from Natchitoches, where there were family properties and where Oscar Chopin established a "General Store." This is the land—Acadie, the low-lying country along the Cane and Red rivers— that provides the setting and materials for the greater part of Kate Chopin's writing. The house in Cloutierville was a comfortably oversized double-verandaed version of the Creole cottage and stood in a pleasant garden among various outbuildings; it was, in fact, the first proper "house" in town, having been built by M. Cloutier himself at the beginning of the century. Inevitably, with its brilliant and spirited mistress, it became a center of social life for the whole district. There is no indication that Kate Chopin suffered from her withdrawal into country life. The detail of her stories is proof that she kept eyes and ears open and relished a variety of human character, masculine and feminine, every bit as colorful and diverse as she had known in St. Louis and New Orleans.

But with her husband's sudden death, from "swamp fever," in the winter of 1882–83, Kate Chopin's life in Cloutierville and Louisiana came abruptly to an end. She elected to return to St. Louis and her mother's house. In 1885 her mother's death left her even more alone, a widow with six young children and no other immediate family. She does not seem to have considered marrying again, though she was later remembered as still, in her widowhood, radiantly attractive. That she turned seriously to writing is not wholly surprising. A family friend and consultant, Dr. Kolbenheyer (model for the unseen advice-giver, Homeyer, in *At Fault*), remembered her vivid letters from Louisiana and apparently urged her to consider putting to use the talent they displayed for observation and characterization. And in the late 1880s the fashion for local-color and regional literature was at its peak. By 1888–89 she was submitting poems and stories to journals around the country. She was soon published in the St. Louis Post-Dispatch, the New Orleans Times-Democrat (where Hearn had been literary editor and taste-maker in the 1880s), in Chicago and Philadelphia papers, and then, most frequently, in the Century, still a magazine of considerable prestige, and in the more popular Vogue and Youth's Companion. By the mid-1890s the Atlantic Monthly, headquarters for the best local-color work, had granted its imprimatur. The first of her two published novels, At Fault, which uses the Cloutierville setting, appeared in 1890—privately printed at her own expense. It was reviewed mostly locally and had no general circulation. But by the time of her two collections of short stories, Bayou Folk (1894; published by the eminently respectable house of Houghton Mifflin) and A Night in Acadie (1897), she was a writer of national reputation.

A consciousness of the risk involved in the theme and plot of her second novel—detailing a woman's "awakening," well after marriage, to the full force of her birthright desire for love and freedom—and the matter-of-fact candor and sensuality of the telling no doubt persuaded her in 1899 to have it published with the mildly avant-garde Chicago firm of Herbert S. Stone, which had bought out Way and Williams, her publisher for A Night in Acadie.[1] For whatever cause—reviewers' and librarians' objections that the book was scandalously immoral, or, just as likely, the possibility that she had poured her own broken and half-buried emotional life into it as into nothing else she had yet written—Kate Chopin's career ended with The Awakening, although a few sketches (one of them the vividly erotic anec-dote, "The Storm") and two longer stories followed during the next year or two. (A third collection of stories had been projected for 1898 and would have included some of her best, such as "A Vocation and a Voice" and the disturbing "Lilacs"; transferred to Herbert Stone, the manuscript was re-turned to the author on the firm's failure in 1900.) The youngest of her

1. She may also have recalled the storm raised by Hardy's Tess and Jude a few years before. One of a series of essays written in 1897 for a St. Louis paper, the Criterion, refers to the scandal of Jude the Obscure, a book Kate Chopin professed to find dull and grotesquely solemn but hardly worth the trouble of hiding from the young. A number of her stories in the 1890s were refused by various editors before getting published—like the extraordinary "A Vocation and a Voice," which William Reedy's St. Louis Mirror finally printed six years after she wrote it. A few never did reach print during her lifetime.

children had now come of age. Though she was barely fifty, her creative energies were spent; and certainly it is easy to imagine how the writing and the reception of *The Awakening* might have been inwardly exhausting. She lived on among friends in the city of her birth, her home being remembered later as nearer to a true salon than any other in St. Louis, but she published almost nothing after 1900. She was delighted by the St. Louis World's Fair of 1904; she bought a season's ticket and went almost daily; and it was after one such daylong visit to the Fair, in August 1904, that she suffered what appears to have been a stroke; though she recovered consciousness briefly and spoke to her children, she died in a coma two days later, at fifty-three.

2

In choosing Creole character and manners as her main subject in fiction, Kate Chopin was following a blazed trail. The stories collected in George Washington Cable's *Old Creole Days* had begun to appear in the mid-1870s, and his melodramatic romance, *The Grandissimes* (1880), had been followed, among other works, by the charming *Bonaventure* (1880), a "prose pastoral" celebrating the custom of life in the Acadian backcountry. In 1888 came the first of Grace King's volumes of Creole stories, set mostly in New Orleans; in 1893, the first collection of Ruth McEnery Stuart's stories of Les Avoyelles Parish (one of Kate Chopin's *Criterion* articles of 1897 is a warm appreciation of Mrs. Stuart's work). The Natchitoches district itself was described from time to time in essays and sketches by "Catherine Cole," another *Times-Democrat* contributor. Among other local-color writers Kate Chopin spoke with approval of the artistry of Sarah Orne Jewett, Mary Eleanor Wilkins (whose 1894 novel, *Pembroke*, was also attacked for "unpleasantness"), and Joel Chandler Harris. But perhaps a more important precedent for her own work was Lafcadio Hearn's *Chita: A Memory of Last Island* (1889), for in the technical virtuosity of Hearn's vivid novella we sense the influence not only of contemporary American magazine practice but of European and specifically French literary standards. Paris, more than New York and Boston—or London—was the point of artistic reference for the European-born Hearn, and it was for Kate Chopin, too. His immediate masters were writers of exotic, heavily atmospheric romance like Gautier and Pierre Loti, while hers were the outwardly more naturalistic *conteurs* such as Daudet and Maupassant (whom she translated); through both streams she would feel the influence of Flaubert, the supreme contemporary example of craftsmanship in fiction.

Kate Chopin's first book, the novel At Fault, is not completely successful, but it displays, at intervals, quite remarkably, a technical sophistication and formed novelistic intelligence that redeem its cursoriness of over-all execution. The main story leans heavily on plot-contrivance and advances by episodic jumps and twists rather than sustained narrative development; thus it is perhaps least effective at its dramatic climax, when the character standing in the way of the protagonists' happiness is conveniently drowned in a rather too patly laid-in flood scene. It is nevertheless a potentially strong and subtle story, and the book as a whole reads as a draft or scenario, with some parts capably filled in, for a novel of genuine power.

The basic situation in At Fault has an element of the autobiographical. The heroine, Thérèse, is a Creole widow who has remained as mistress of her Cane River establishment (as the widow of Oscar Chopin did not). Expectably the story ends in her remarriage; but in working out a narrative scheme that both offers her this possibility and puts a particular concentration of obstacles in the way of realizing it, Kate Chopin reached beyond romantic sentiment to a moral theme of great resonance. It is the theme of selfishness and what we might call self-generosity—that living from within one's own deeper being that alone makes living-for-others a life-giving act. What at first blocks Thérèse's remarrying is the fact of her "American" lover's ill-considered first marriage to a pitiful, vulgar "American" girl with whom he had soon found that he had nothing in common and whom he had permitted to divorce him after discovering that she had become a closet alcoholic. Yet it is not so much the divorce that comes between the lovers— though the "prejudices of a Catholic education" are given their due—as the sense that Hosmer had failed to give his weak-natured wife the moral support she had needed; and Thérèse's challenge to Hosmer's "manhood" is to "face the consequences of his own actions." But in time Thérèse must face the consequences of her own more subtly destructive highmindedness, for she has thus condemned Hosmer to an ordeal, in renewing an irretrievable marriage, that is a death sentence to his spirit. The subplot involving Hosmer's sister, Melicent, and Thérèse's nephew Grégoire Santien, mirrors the main story; Melicent, described as a girl who can "look after herself," plays at being in love with Grégoire but has already rejected—as something that "could not be thought of"—the possibility of actually giving herself in love and marriage to this odd-speaking Creole (his foreignness seems to her a kind of "physical deformation" that is nevertheless oddly fascinating;

somehow it appears "not to detract from a definite inheritance of good breeding").

Grégoire is the first in a sizeable company of rough-diamond Creole heroes in Kate Chopin's work, men whose aristocratic purity of spirit is masked behind a thick dialect and rough manners; they live always close to their passions, sure of their place in the world but without pretense or snobbery. In *At Fault* Grégoire moves between childlike simplicity—in love, in despair—and cold violence, shooting down without a tremor of remorse a halfbreed malcontent whom he catches setting fire to Hosmer's mill, and later getting himself killed in a pointless frontier quarrel of honor. His mistreatment by Melicent Hosmer is part of a more general pattern of contrasts between "American" and Creole behavior. The novel somewhat awkwardly turns aside for chapters of coarse-grained caricature showing life among several social-climbing "American" ladies (speaking a remarkable early variety of beauty-parlor slang) who represent the social world Hosmer is trying to put behind him, a world in comparison with which the natural warmth and generosity of Creole manners can only gain in attractiveness.[2] These folklore contrasts might appear forced and mechanical. What secures their effectiveness, and what puts the breath of real life into that intermittent sequence of developed scenes that does draw us into the story, is Kate Chopin's ability to make almost tangible the bodily presence people have for each other, and the charm of life, or the wretchedness, that radiates physically out of them. We feel this power, one she shares with the greatest masters of fiction, in the slightest details and images—Thérèse's bare forearm reaching across the papers on Hosmer's desk; her unguarded physical tenderness with Hosmer's peevish wife; Hosmer brooding alone "like a man who has been stricken" in the trap of his remarriage—details that invariably endorse the novel's moral theme.

Two particular talents are apparent in the construction of *At Fault*, though they do not fuse compositionally. One is for devising a suitably elaborate chronicle of interlaced lives and destinies bearing on a steady central theme; the other is for the intensive presentation of troubled personal histories, suffering and yet not without a power to react upon circumstance. (The essential submissiveness of Dreiser's best characters, the mechanical desolation-equations that are imposed on Edith Wharton's, are not the behavioral rule here.) On the whole it is the second talent that flourishes in Kate

2. One scene built around this opposition—between the "American" girl, Lucilla, a pale, drooping, stuck-up religious prig, and her unaffected Creole counterpart, Ninette Duplan (Part II, chapter 11)—makes a fine comic interlude.

Chopin's subsequent work. Her one other published novel, *The Awakening*, narrows its focus to the history of a single main character. Yet a certain density and solidity of social background are never absent. She regularly backs her stories, even the briefest, with those "flashes out of a community life" that Sherwood Anderson would later define as the further truthfulness he was reaching for in his. One chapter in *At Fault* (Part II, chapter 8) is a piece of indirect narration—refracting an episode in the main story through a comic retelling of it, in dialect, by a houseful of supernumeraries—that Mark Twain, or Faulkner, would have been proud of.[3] The occasional reappearance of characters central to one story as accessory figures in another adds to this impression that a whole society and its inner history are being brought to life.

The first three stories in *Bayou Folk* concern Grégoire Santien and his two brothers, quixotically virtuous descendants of one of the great Creole plantation families ruined in the Civil War. These stories, and most of the briefer tales that follow, appeal unembarrassedly to sentiment and usually end with some more or less melodramatic formula of revelation or reversal. But these are not necessarily crippling flaws in storytelling. It is possible to be sentimental with situations and yet clear-eyed and firm with the attendant emotions; and it is in handling the common life of natural emotion that Kate Chopin is strongest, unfailingly direct. Her Creoles, Cajuns, and patois-speaking negroes are full of venial sins of the most familiar kind; they smoke (the women, too), use wine, eat well—or complain when they don't; are covetous, stubborn, lazy, inconsolable, self-frustrating, splendidly irrational, and keep, the best of them, an instinctive courtesy and dignity in the face of deprivation or others' meanness; in short, they are fairly unintelligible by "American" and Protestant standards of conduct.

They are also invariably felt as real physical presences. A half paragraph in "In Sabine" gives us a touch, again, of this Tolstoyan physicality that is Kate Chopin's particular gift:

> Grégoire loved women. He liked their nearness, their atmosphere;
> the tones of their voices and the things they said; their ways of

3. A reader of Kate Chopin may come to be slightly haunted by anticipations of later American storytelling. A sketch, "Juanita," not included in her two published collections, looks ahead to the scheme of Carson McCullers's "Ballad of the Sad Cafe"; the confused yearning of the heroine of "A Respectable Woman" is rendered in the very idiom of *Winesburg, Ohio*; the self-absorption of a beach party of comic types (*The Awakening*, chapter 12) seems purest Eudora Welty, while another set piece of narrative refraction in *At Fault* (Part II, chapter 12) projects a figure straight out of the coolly murderous Texas of Katherine Anne Porter's "Noon Wine."

moving and turning about; the brushing of their garments when they passed by him pleased him. He was fleeing now from the pain that a woman had inflicted upon him. . . .

A few stories in *Bayou Folk* develop tragically, like "La Belle Zoraïde." Nearly all carry a suggestion that people, however grotesque or foolish, are to be helped and pitied, and that to expect to get through life free of sorrow, or loss, or despair is hardly within reason. Kate Chopin has this rare truthfulness among storytellers: she knows fairly precisely how difficult life is and how commonplace its tragedies, yet also how something in us that is equally uncontrollable—a kind of indifference to moral sums, a numbness to demonstrated probabilities, the irrepressible reawakening of some familiar expectation of pleasure—can turn us toward it again almost despite ourselves. One feels sometimes that finishing her stories bores her a little. The pivotal moments of feeling, the revelations of essential character-states, are the great thing. How she would have enjoyed *Dubliners*—an even better model for her talent than Maupassant (and itself deriving, like her own work, from French precedents).

Most of the stories in *A Night in Acadie*, her third book, are entertainments. But two at least strike deeper emotionally: "Athénaïse," telling of a girl's premature marriage (one emblem for which is a striking memory-image of chattel slavery) and her release into the happiness of adult sensuousness and passion; and "At Chênière Caminada," in which the frustration of hopeless love is given a terrible, dehumanizing force. The core themes of these two mid-1890s stories come together in *The Awakening*, by common agreement Kate Chopin's finest book and one of the few wholly adult novels in our older literature. But *The Awakening* is something more than a study of a woman's liberation into sensuality and personal freedom out of the constrictions of her life as a leisure-class wife and mother.[4] If it were only that, it might not have been so deeply scandalous—for the novel of physical passion and release in women characters was itself becoming a literary convention in the late 1880s and 1890s, however repugnant to politer tastes. What distinguishes Kate Chopin's book from Mrs. Amélie Rives-Chanler's *The Quick or the Dead?*, Miss Curry's *Bohemian Tragedy*, Laura Daintrey's *Eros*, Gertrude Atherton's *What Dreams May Come*, Elizabeth Robins's *The Open Question*, and the like, is what distinguished Hardy's *Tess of the*

---

4. Recent feminist readings of *The Awakening*, in their eagerness to add this novel's testimony to an altogether valid political agenda, have rather underrated, I think, its actual power.

D'Urbervilles: an artistic intensity and concentration that release its emotional content with irreversible force, and then, also, a disturbing element of submission and compliance in the telling, an absorption in the story at each stage of it that defers to no law or scruple except that of its own relentless progression.

All Kate Chopin's ordinary skill in developing atmosphere and scene, and in presenting her characters as sensually alive to one another, goes into the writing of *The Awakening*. But the pull of the story toward dissolution and catastrophe finally transcends these vivifying particulars. Some destructive power in existence that is stronger than love or shame or comfort or self-interest or even a woman's spontaneous delight in her children (a counter-force rendered in the book without sentimentality) rises in the last chapters and rages, as it seems, out of control. *The Awakening* quite possibly *is* an immoral, or demoralizing, book, in the way that, say, Camus' *Stranger* has been accused of being demoralizing. In a mock apology to her critics published a few months after the novel was issued, Kate Chopin claimed that the story had taken her by surprise; she had never dreamed of her heroine's "making such a mess of things and working out her own damnation as she did." There are indications that this account of the matter was not altogether ironical. A diary note from 1894 opens the door for a moment on changes of spirit and of self-understanding the full history of which can only be guessed at; it connects her "past ten years of growth—my real growth" to some deadly effacement of her dearest past associations that she cannot wholly comprehend. And in the novel itself a real tiredness and despair of life are strongly asserted in the closing episodes; a stupor at "the great unnumbered multitude of souls that come and go"; a despondency that finally does not lift. It is perhaps only with the most intensely imagined art that we feel this particular ambiguity: that at the core there is an intensely personal message, but that the work as a whole resists our interpreting it autobiographically. What we do know is simply that *The Awakening* imposes its story on us with, in the end, unusual authority—and that after its publication, and its public mauling by reviewers and other opinion-makers, Kate Chopin would have, as a writer, very little more to say.

6

O. Henry

His Life and Afterlife

In 1916, six years after the much lamented death, at forty-eight, of the popular storyteller who called himself "O. Henry," a biography appeared—delayed for several years by the death of the man originally assigned to write it but kept afloat as a project by O. Henry's devoted publisher, Doubleday, Page and Company, who among other motives saw it as a means of recovering the sizeable advances outstanding at the writer's death. The book that resulted, a nonfictional romance credited to a certain C. Alphonso Smith and published under the curious title O. *Henry Biography*, reaches one rousing climax in a paragraph close early in its seventh chapter: "If ever in American literature the place and the man met, they met when O. Henry strolled for the first time along the streets of New York." It is a sentence marking with due emphasis the moment of impending triumph, after many troubles and reverses, that the book's first audience would have been confidently anticipating. The implication is clear. To bring about this happy convergence of man and milieu, a special providence must have been at work. So, anciently, saints' lives were written, making full use of the darker hours before some great soul's recovery and ascent; so, too, in our day, the life stories of Hollywood luminaries, rock stars, geniuses from the advertising and fashion trades.

The author, however, of this oddly baptized book—can we imagine other titles using the same formula: *Jennie Gerhardt Novel* perhaps, or "Alfred Prufrock Poem"?—was no mere publicist or penny-a-liner. On the title page he is identified as Poe Professor of English at the University of Virginia and author of, among other works, a volume called *What Can Literature Do for Me?* ("It Can Give You an Outlet," the answer begins, and continues: "It Can Keep Before You the Vision of the Ideal," "It Can Show You the Glory of the Commonplace," "It Can Give You Mastery of Your Own Language.") For the job of memorializing a writer who at his death was being described not merely by his publishers but by ranking literary arbiters as the successor in American fiction to Poe and Hawthorne, and the peer of Hardy, Henry James, and Rudyard Kipling (first English-language recipient, three years before, of the new Nobel Prize in Literature), two things in particular would have recommended Professor Smith. Having written early in his academic life on respectable subjects in philology and poetics—his Johns Hopkins thesis, *The Order of Words in Anglo-Saxon Prose* (1893), was followed by *Repetition and Parallelism in English Verse* (1894) and *An Old English Grammar* (1896)—he had lately, as Roosevelt Professor of American history and institutions at the University of Berlin during 1910–11, lectured on the American short story and produced a compact guide for German readers, *Die Amerikanische Literatur* (1912). Also he was a fellow townsman. Two years the junior of William Sydney Porter, O. Henry's widely known real name, Professor Smith had grown up with him in Greensboro, North Carolina; had walked the same streets, attended the same school, shopped at the pharmacy where Will Porter clerked from his sixteenth to his twentieth year while growing locally famous for drawing genial, dead-accurate cartoons of Greensboro's citizenry; and in the process had soaked in all those influences of Southern town life during the post–Civil War era without which, he was sure, Will Porter "would hardly have developed into the O. Henry that we know to-day."

Smith's biography maintains the double perspective of these credentials. On the one hand, responsible critical and historical judgments are assumed to be in order and are not lacking. The book opens with an analysis of the basic structure of an O. Henry story as it makes its play for the reader's attention—a structure seen as strangely coincident with the four distinct stages of O. Henry's own "romantic career." Later passages speak in turn of the writer's favorite subjects and themes; of the characteristic "beauty of style," mastery of "significant detail," and "exuberance of color"; of the "trick of the diverted and diverting quotation," or deliberate misquotation, to amuse his more educated readers; of a psychological acumen held to rival central insights of Professor William James himself (identified early on as a fervent admirer); of a "mingled sympathy and indignation"—and of course humor—"that recall Dickens on every page"; and most of all of an organic vision of human society in the new metropolitan era, a vision enabling O. Henry "to get closer to the inner life of the great city and to succeed better in giving it a voice than any one else had done." (Dreiser's name, it goes without saying, does not appear, and Whitman's does only in a list of American classics compiled by a foreign observer.) The renowned technique is given its due: the neatly balanced narrative ironies, the endings that surprise chiefly by virtue of their momentarily concealed inevitability. But technique is not all, Professor Smith insists. Technique, at most, "bares and vivifies." Rather, it is theme that works deepest into the reader's mind and feeling. And here is the special distinction that gives O. Henry his place in the pantheon of national literary accomplishment: "In his hands the short story has become the organ of a social consciousness more varied and multiform than it had ever expressed before." Professor Smith is categorical on this point. Washington Irving, he concludes, "legendized" the short story, Poe "standardized" it, Hawthorne "allegorized" it, Bret Harte "local-ized" it; but O. Henry, out of an unrivaled familiarity with the entire spectrum of popular American life, has "humanized" it.

In re-creating the years leading up to O. Henry's New York triumphs, Professor Smith writes quite explicitly from the perspective of "those of us who remained in the home town"; those who, because they knew him when, can best understand and appreciate all the intervening developments. It is worth remembering that when Smith wrote his book there was still considerable scandal surrounding the pseudonym "O. Henry," and a good deal in William Sydney Porter's life still to explain, and explain away. Above all, there was the notorious episode of his three-year term in the Ohio Federal Penitentiary for the double felony of embezzlement and running from justice (he had fled the country and holed up in Honduras for several months before returning to face trial). The biography thus becomes a final rehabilitation and act of reparation. Forthrightly addressed, this mysterious lapse in a great career—and what more alarming crime could there be in the Horatio Alger epoch than a young man's apparent betrayal of both financial and juridical trust?—loses its taint of dishonor and is subsumed within a larger, implicitly heroic pattern of ordeal and transcendence.

In Smith's narrative, as in one of Edwin Arlington Robinson's town-focused poems from the same epoch, like "Flammonde" or "Richard Cory" (but with a happier ending), some "we" is looking wonderingly at an already legendary "him." No stance could have appealed more effectively to the book's captive readership, that McKinley-to-Harding–era public whose appetite for processed accounts of the more consoling sorts of human difficulty O. Henry's storytelling had perfectly taken the measure of. Professor Smith's own genial legendizing follows suit. At every stage the hero's life and character prove to be the stuff of popular myth. As a boy he is a match at chess for anyone in town; he is also a skillful boxer (years later, in prison, he will floor with one punch an enraged bull of a convict threatening mayhem to the penitentiary doctor), a "trained fencer," a champion roller-skater. At school he is remembered as writing his lesson with one hand while simultaneously executing caricatures of the teacher with the other. In speech and behavior he is gentle, delicate, "absolutely without malice," yet never "sissy." In wild Texas he effortlessly acquires fluent Spanish, both the Mexican and the Castilian varieties; he outdoes veteran cowboys as bronco-buster and crack shot; he is equally proficient as a ranch cook; he learns bookkeeping with phenomenal ease and rapidity; in the free-for-all of frontier conversation he is witty and brilliant, yet his jokes are never vulgar. He is above all a genuine democrat whose power to absorb and re-create the life around him comes from a perfect equability and a fine unconcern for the invidious contemporary ethos of class exclusiveness and social discrimination. On the staff of the *Houston Daily Post* in the mid-1890s he becomes the most popular employee; his editor, having already nearly doubled his salary, reluctantly but honorably urges him to seek the fortune he merits, in New York. It is recalled that he did have "one great failing"—"an inability to say 'No' to any man"—and so we are prepared for the fateful episode of the shortfall in his accounts as teller in an Austin, Texas, bank.

But in the "shadowed years" that now follow, his essential character is seen to hold firm. With pharmacy skills retrieved from an industrious boyhood, Will Porter saves the prison warden from accidental poisoning, and is vouched for as a spotless soul and compassionate friend by no less an authority than one Al Jennings, the notorious train robber. Friends and family play out their roles in comparable ways. For the fidelity of his wife's parents at the time of his imprisonment only the idiom of Scripture will suffice: "their love for him knew no waning and their faith in him neither variableness nor the shadow of turning." The mythic pattern of ordeal and triumph carries over into the years of fame. He arrives in New York unannounced and all but unknown, like Childe Roland coming to the Dark Tower. Once established, he modestly resists lionizing, forces himself on no man, gives away his money as freely as, in conversation, his inexhaustible charm and humor. And he remains, as ever, a democrat and humanitarian, discovering in story after story—Professor Smith resorts to Dickensian iteration to make the point—"those common traits and common impulses which together form a sort of common denominator of our common humanity."

So the life and character of O. Henry are displayed to us in the perspective of 1916, his biographer confident of the strength and permanence of his creative achievement. Soon enough the bubble burst. The oversold reputation went into a rapid and, to date, unreversed decline; not, however, before giving a name (and whose better?) to an annual selection of magazine writing published as the O. Henry Memorial Award Prize Stories. The newspaper-smart jocularity of style—which, in the wake of admired practitioners like Bill Nye and Eugene Field, O. Henry finished domesticating from its rougher origins in the popular humor of the 1850s—came to be recognized for what it was: the pinched middle-class soul's protective charm against an energy and a wisdom in life too intimidating to risk direct commerce with, a talisman against every profounder human passion. The same may be said of an essential and inveterate condescension toward the actors in his stories—though we recognize how well this answered to the depths of uneasy condescension in his readership in an era preoccupied with finding out precisely whom one might consort with socially without damage to one's reputation or credit standing; an era and a readership highly vulnerable, therefore, to stories expressing a measured sympathy for all those (as Professor Smith elegantly phrases it) "of whatever age or sex, who work at tasks not commonly rated as cultural." It is a style and narrative attitude that, apart from the parody versions concocted by Perelman and Thurber, Ring Lardner and Nathanael West, would find its natural home half a century later in the routines of "situation" comedy. (Appropriately an O. Henry Television Playhouse enjoyed a brief run during the 1950s, in commercial television's apprentice years.) Need one look further than Neil

Simon for a contemporary equivalent to O. Henry's extraordinary popular success as chronicler, *mutatis mutandis*, of New York "life"?

Arriving at such up-to-date comparisons, we may in fact begin to think a little better of O. Henry's achievement as a storyteller, or at least acknowledge the resourcefulness of it according to its time and place. Admittedly the passages introduced by Professor Smith to illustrate beauty of style, penetration of the humbler secrets of city life, the ring of true steel as the narrative lock closes, or some underlying though disregarded truth about human existence, are now mostly embarrassing to read through (" 'Oh, I reckon you'd have ended up about the same,' said Bob Tidball, cheerfully philosophical. 'It ain't the roads we take; it's what's inside us that makes us turn out the way we do.' "). Nevertheless, it is to O. Henry's credit that, commanding a large popular audience, he did write about the "Four Million" rather than the "Four Hundred"; about—like Dreiser after all—embattled shopgirls, struggling immigrants, down-and-outers, jailbirds, and ordinary men and women coping as best they can with defeat and loss, injury and insult. Professor Smith quotes, early along, a contemporary judgment of O. Henry's storytelling "charm" as consisting of "three parts softness" and of the writer himself as a "soft-hearted advocate of humanity." There are, unfortunately, worse things for a skillful popular writer to become.

Indeed, at a time when serious literary commentary, reverting once more to a guardian's moral strictness, has grown oddly suspicious of fiction-making of any kind, and when we find the allegedly neutral and scientific term "manipulation" proposed as an all-purpose substitute for the older studio term "handling," the very overmanagement for which O. Henry became a byword may reemerge as a quality fundamental to the problematic art in question. The *New York Sun*'s claim, in 1915, that he was a "writer's writer" might thus point to a significant critical truth, quite apart from our recognizing that in both subject matter and style O. Henry prepared not a little of the ground for the *New Yorker* storytellers of the 1920s and 1930s, to say nothing of the eminently magazinish talent of a Scott Fitzgerald. The best subsequent critical introduction, Eugene Current-Garcia's volume for the Twayne United States Author Series (1965), has made the point that it was precisely O. Henry's exemplary "dexterity in ordering and controlling his materials" that won him the admiration of French readers. One among these, Raoul Narcy, in an article reprinted in *The Living Age* in 1919, defined his strength in terms that sound surprisingly contemporary—for in saying of a writer that "he dominates his characters rather than suffering them," isn't one saying that he is essentially an *auteur*; that is, a creator

who satisfies us precisely because he never wholly surrenders his imaginative will to the situations in life that are ostensibly being treated? In this view the very implausibility and manipulativeness of O. Henry's fiction only emphasize his impudent command of the whole performative occasion, the "scene of writing" itself (in our later idiom). Practitioners of *nouvelle critique* regularly build their anthropological arguments on the formulaic structures, or power trips, of detective stories and science fiction; the more formulaic, the better. One may be surprised that they have not yet rediscovered O. Henry's unvarying art.

Of such critical fancifulness C. Alphonso Smith was agreeably innocent. The final note in his accounting is as hagiographic as the rest; in the closing paragraph of the biography we are told about an unidentified woman whose life had been touched in some unknown fashion by O. Henry's humane genius and who, after his funeral, "was seen to remain alone kneeling in prayer." For the reader who wants more detailed information about O. Henry's actual literary career, including the findings (and dismissals) of another half-century of intermittent scholarship, Professor Current-Garcia's book is more substantially serviceable. But Professor Smith's, in its way, is indispensable. It stands in relation to the case of O. Henry somewhat as Albert Bigelow Paine's biography does to the grander history and career of Mark Twain; that is, having been written when the living presence of its subject was still abroad in the land, it is where students of the whole curious history can profitably start.

7

Modern Instances

Brooks, Mumford, Dreiser

The Mutual Admiration Pact
of Van Wyck Brooks and Lewis Mumford

Van Wyck Brooks (1886–1963) and Lewis Mumford (1895–1990) were close
friends and correspondents for more than forty years and major participants
in the campaign for cultural "renewal" that played so large a part in the
effort of American men of letters following World War I.[1] "Quite spontane-
ously," Mumford writes of their early association, "we became fellow workers
on the task of reclaiming our American literary heritage"; and while his
own concerns as a writer broadened to embrace the whole development of

---

1. *The Van Wyck Brooks, Lewis Mumford Letters: The Record of a Literary Friendship, 1921–1963,*
edited by Robert E. Spiller (New York: E. P. Dutton, 1970).

modern Western civilization and the deepening crisis of its twentieth-century self-ravagement, he remained so much the more intensely faithful to the idea of redeeming present and future through an expanded understanding, an appreciation both humane and aggressively rational, of the traceable past. The mood of much of their correspondence—certain always of the public importance of what each was doing, and marble-constant in championing liberal-humanistic values and goals—is one that now may be harder and harder to recall or to imagine steadfastly basing daily choices upon, let alone a lifelong career in the making of books. But that should only increase interest in what these letters have to show and the light they possibly cast on a literary epoch whose inventiveness and productivity still astonish us and whose life-records are only beginning to be assembled systematically.

[It must be said that the scholarly editing of the present volume sets a poor precedent for serving this interest. An ominous sentence in the editor's preface tells us that the letters we are about to read "have been chosen, cut, arranged, and paragraphed" so as to tell "a single connected story" of world-shaking intellectual exploration. This may mean much or little in the way of editorial interference, but confidence in the project is not bolstered by obvious errors in transcription and by the waywardness of the indexing and annotation. To take a single case of a botched name, it cannot have been the meticulous Brooks who urged his friend, in a letter singled out as one of the most important in the lot, to read a French moralist named "Vanvenvargues," the index here merely deepening the mystery with an entry on a certain "Marquis de Vanvargues." Doubts about the editor's principle of selection from a correspondence preserved, he says, in its entirety increase sharply when, following up Mumford's pointed comment in 1962 on the great value to future scholars of a letter of Brooks's written in April 1925, we discover that this particular letter has not been included. Perhaps it all goes to justify, ironically, a series of jibes against the tribe of professors, especially literature professors, forming a conspicuous subtheme in both men's letters.]

The bulk of their correspondence, as here presented, is occupied more with the ceremonies of comradeship than with arguing out new lines of thought. There are reports of work in progress, the reception of completed books and fresh plans for the future; messages of congratulations and fraternal support; accounts of the comings and goings of common friends, of travel and new domestic arrangements, of business at the National Institute of Arts and Letters in New York, and, during World War II, of committees

and propaganda campaigns to redirect national opinion. The war dominates the middle stretches of the volume. Its tensions, in fact, pushed to the brink of open antagonism certain differences in outlook and personal style that elsewhere served as a convenient basis for mutual admiration (each man responding to abilities in the other that he could accept, through lack of interest, his own deficiency in); for it was during World War II and its uncertain aftermath that Mumford's combative fervor and Brooks's radical innocence about public affairs brought them out at irreconcilable cross-purposes, as on the issue of aid to Britain in 1941 (before Pearl Harbor) or, in 1948, the granting of a medal for distinguished literary service to the unrepentant isolationist Charles Beard. Here Mumford's characteristic violence of feeling carried them as close to an irreparable break as they ever came, and needlessly so (as Mumford later acknowledged). In the long run, despite Brooks's customary deference to his friend's judgment in political matters, his own casual instinct that Beard's politics were to be explained by his being "at bottom an Indiana farmer" seems more in the path of wisdom than Mumford's intemperate denunciation of the man as "an intellectual Quisling" who was responsible for making a whole younger generation of Americans "indifferent to human values."

Their near quarrel blew over quickly and left no great trace, but the best days of their literary comradeship had ended. The inward disappointment each was now haunted by, facing increasingly unsympathetic or indifferent reviews and the evident failure of his magnum opus to change opinion in the way intended, turns the last stages of their correspondence into little more than an exchange of sympathies, complaints, and personal blessings. Rather than these inevitable later moments of anger and diminished expectancy, one prefers to remember earlier and braver times—the zest and courage with which they launched their most ambitious undertakings, or that quite extraordinary kindness and intelligence of consideration Mumford showed Brooks during his prolonged breakdown in the late 1920s; the younger man's wise insistence, emphasizing the solid work Brooks had already done rather than the fears and doubts that were preventing its continuance, on the essential "soundness and integrity of Van Wyck's life," and his highly effective practical help in getting Brooks back in harness and the blocked life of Emerson into print and out of the way.

The real value of this collection of private letters is in directing us back to the published work that stands as the legacy of these two remarkable literary lives. To me the correspondence, particularly as it moves into the era of World War II, recalls a good deal of my own first coming-of-age as

student and citizen, when both men had an important place among the
multitude of my teachers (though never the most important). Reading their
letters has set me rereading their books, in the fresh light of their own
conception of them, and the results have been just a little surprising.
Mumford's was clearly the stronger, the more adventurous and versatile
mind; a tacit acceptance of this superiority is in fact one of the ruling
fictions of their correspondence. (You are the one living American, Brooks
writes, "capable of the monumental, the classic thing" [1931]; "the chosen
man of our time to be the giver of laws" [1944]; "one of the world minds
who are going to be recognized everywhere as a pillar of the Age of
Reconstruction" [1946], offering fundamental clarification "on these great
all-human questions—marriage, sex—etc. etc." [1952]). But Brooks seems
now, as I reread them, to be the true writer of the pair. It is his work that at
its best is still expressively alive and has caught the life in those subjects
lying nearest the writer's heart.

To formulate the matter all too bluntly, Mumford strikes one, in the mass
of his work, as essentially not a writer at all—and not a philosopher either—
but a man of action, a framer and executer of campaigns and programs. (His
best writing, I would argue, is in his architectural journalism—his fine essay-
review on Frank Lloyd Wright, for example, when the new Guggenheim
Museum was beginning to be built—and his vigorously polemical surveys of
postwar urban expansion, new housing and expressway schemes, and the
whole panorama of contemporary civic design; by all report he seems, too,
to have been an inspiring lecturer and teacher.) Mumford's intelligence is
practical-prophetic, his thinking controlled by a determination to maintain
a workable opening for public action. He came early to a strong period
intuition (it was the era of Spengler's *Decline of the West*) that Western
society was already far gone into revolutionary transformations which would
either "displace a mean and inferior kind of life" with something "completely different" or else destroy it altogether (1925), and this intuition—
abundantly endorsed by his time's history—would serve him as a lifelong
basis for practical criticism and vast evangelical recommendations for
change. He did in fact perform public service of genuine value on the New
York City school board in the 1930s and on any number of committees and
commissions, but to my mind the place that would have put to the very best
use his exceptional talents and energies is the one that was held through
most of his adult life by Robert Moses, the Supreme Antagonist of so many
of Mumford's humane diatribes against metropolitan sprawl. His purposes as
a writer are invariably subordinated to some grand effort at reshaping public

consciousness. The way he speaks of his books in these letters is indicative. His first book, a historical study of utopias, is undertaken because "it seemed to me necessary to throw a rainbow into the sky at just this moment" (1922), i.e., in the gloom of the early post-Versailles years. *Technics and Civilization*, the first volume of the great philosophical work he means to leave as his masterpiece, is announced as "a grand broadside at the mechanists and the mammonists from within their citadel" (1933); and the moment has come to begin the final volume, he feels, when his combative energies have surged back and he finds himself "in a working and fighting mood: ready to leave despair to the young" (1945).

He is, in a word, a pamphleteer. His ideas about human civilization are instruments to him, simple and all compact, that he deploys for the purpose of assailing the minds, the working prejudices, of other people. As early as *The Golden Day* (1926), that perceptive man Waldo Frank caught something fundamental to the case in remarking that Mumford was somehow "outside the historical experience he describes and celebrates"; "he has gone deep to behold our past greatness, our present miseries, but not deep enough to establish the vital connection between them and between them and himself." The result is the odd combination of cursoriness and repetitiveness, the overstatement and the oversimplification, the monotonous overinsistence of voice, that in the long run betray his learning and high purpose to a kind of noble crankishness. What he wrote, toward the end of *The Condition of Man* (1944), about his old teacher Patrick Geddes summarizes his own case as well: that Geddes had sacrificed to "citizenship" and a syncretistic conception of universal human renewal his individual chances at success and mastery in any particular task. For Mumford, too, this was an honorable sacrifice, but his books are its victims.[2]

Brooks for his part repeatedly confesses that he has no head at all for these grandiose speculations. His 1952 essay on Mumford (reprinted in *The Writer in America*) is all generous acquiescence and praise. But the remarkable revelation of these letters is that on the rare occasions when he subjected his friend's writing to detached criticism, he spoke directly to its *literary* weakness. In a long letter about *The Brown Decades* (1931), Brooks

---

2. "Crankish" is a harsh word, yet not inappropriate for a writer who, in *The Condition of Man*, could fix the climax of his panoramic survey of the advance of Western civilization, and the starting point for the creation of a redemptive "world culture," in the emergence of his teacher (Geddes being "the Bacon and the Leonardo, perhaps the Galileo" of the time to come). The whole book is a monument to its author's intellectual vigor, but as a piece of writing it is of the type of Will Durant's capable popularizations rather than an advancement of historical understanding.

commented on a rhetorical fault in Mumford's work that in effect compromised the very truth of his argument; it was his way of addressing himself to
"some 'central,' hypothetical audience, which in your mind you assume
should exist, but which really doesn't exist and will not exist . . . until it has
been created by some [great] critical historian"—precisely the kind of
authoritative historian Mumford was too impatient to become. This letter,
Mumford replied, had stirred him deeply, setting him the great challenge he
would devote the next twenty years to answering. But when, exactly twenty
years later, Brooks offered a fresh "word of counsel" that once again struck
at the whole basis of Mumford's performance, it was too late for Mumford to
be anything but, on the point at issue, stupefied and grieved. Reading
through the run of his friend's books in order to write his essay about them,
Brooks had become sensitive to the abstractness and tonal flatness of
Mumford's style and had recommended, as a saving refreshment, that
Mumford spend a sort of sabbatical year reading the old literary moralists,
Emerson, La Bruyère, and the like; writers, we would all say, whose
sentences and paragraphs keep close to the concrete rhythms and details of
felt human experience. "Whom on earth do you think I read every day of
my life?" Mumford fired back—once again, with his grammatical fussiness,
shooting himself in the stylistic foot. The point was shrewdly taken, though
Brooks had no stomach for pressing it and backed off in his next letter with
many apologies. The intellectual authority of the writers he had in mind he
knew to be inseparable from their mastery of expression, and on that testing
ground his friend's great message was doomed to go unheard.

Past his first rebellious youth ideas were hardly more than names to
Brooks, good or bad according to the character and reputation of their
proponents. As a practical critic he appears mainly as a connoisseur of that
"beautiful writing," whatever it might be about, which in the sourer moods
of his later years he was convinced no longer counted for anything in
reigning critical circles. What fascinated him were the lives and everyday
personalities of the people who write books. ("I am as curious about them
as a puppy is about other dogs," he once beguilingly remarked.) Thus,
memoirs, journals, letters, and reported conversations meant as much to
him as major artistic creations. One consequence of this is the *critical*
unsatisfactoriness of his treatment of the greatest writers and books—his
multivolumed panorama of the literary history of the United States can tell
you almost everything about the periods and movements under discussion
except why their masterpieces (if they produced any) are indeed masterpieces, and by what rare effort of will and disciplined imagination these

came to be written—but another consequence is the sympathetic charm and vividness of his portraits of lesser figures and their working milieux. Here it was enough for him to write *con amore*, or (his own phrase) "from the innards." He is never farther from Mumford's oppressive sense of mission than when he remarks (1944) that it is bad for him to talk about subjects he is at work on, since "what I really do mean I never know till I've written it out." There speaks the instinctive writer, though perhaps the unrescuably minor one.

With subjects that do not disturb his uncritical idealism and that he can tolerate imaginatively as human experiences, it becomes for Brooks a matter of strength rather than weakness that, as he once candidly admitted, "writing has always been my secret asylum," the regular means of saving himself from some fearful inward dislocation, some looming idiocy of empty-mindedness. At the close of *Days of the Phoenix*, the second of the three volumes of recollections that make up his *Autobiography*, he asserts that "all writers . . . exist under a sort of spell or, one might say, within a magic circle" which must remain largely unbroken if they are to get through their work. That, of course, is not the whole truth about literature, but it is a part of the whole truth; and Brooks's vast elaboration of it in his memoirs of the lives of writers and artists remains a contribution of permanent value.

Robert Penn Warren's Dreiser

Theodore Dreiser stands as the extreme case of a phenomenon peculiar to the novel as a literary form: that it is possible to write with, sentence by sentence, a teeth-grinding infelicity of style and yet have the authority, the power to change and deepen awareness, of a master. Against assurances by native speakers that Dostoevsky's prose is crudely journalistic or that Silone "simply doesn't *write* well," the answer has to be that such judgments are beside the point. In an extended work of circumstantial prose narration, the decisive units of effectiveness are something other than the individual sentence or paragraph. As regards style, novels (so Marvin Mudrick has put it, in an essay on *character* and *event* in prose fiction) need only be just well enough written. What matters, besides a certain seriousness of conception, is the sustained impression of living personality, the weight and momentum of the developed narrative illusion, the imaginative sequences and progressions of the whole—but these achievements are famously the hardest things in major literature to get defined to the satisfaction of nonbelievers.

In Dreiser's case it is not really surprising that his least apologetic admirers, from Ford Madox Ford and H. G. Wells to Saul Bellow and Robert Penn Warren, have mostly been other novelists, a class of readers less easily distracted by preconceptions and quickest to recognize authority when they come upon it. Not only other lead-footed Chicago naturalists but writers identified with craftsmanship and critical sophistication have spoken up for Dreiser. You would expect to find James Farrell and Nelson Algren in his camp but not, offhand, the author of *The Good Soldier* or the *Fugitives*-bred poet and man of letters whose textbooks, in collaboration with Cleanth Brooks, imposed on a whole generation of teachers and students the dogma that no literary promise was worth much that was not technically fulfilled. Paradoxically Dreiser, first famous as a *cause célèbre* (through the luck of censorship and prosecution) in an era aggressively committed to cultural liberation, holds his place now as a novelist's novelist. All he does well is the elusive essential thing: he tells a compelling story and persuades us that it happens in a real, humanly consequential world.

Robert Penn Warren's centennial tribute, *Homage to Theodore Dreiser* (1971), is an expansion of his *Yale Review* essay on *An American Tragedy* of ten years earlier. The section on this novel remains the best and central part. It is with *An American Tragedy*, for example, that Warren specifies some of the other formal "languages," besides that of words and sentences, that create fictional meaning—"the language of unfolding scenes"; "the language of the imagery of enactment, with all its primitive massiveness"; the language of multiple and shifting "perspectives," through a simple abundance of analogous characterizations and scenes, by which a story comes to seem inclusive and irreversible; the all but indefinable symbolism of "pause and acceleration" in the main action, of "approach and with-drawal" in the relations of action and character, and of rhythmic alterations between the establishment and the unmasking of fundamental "illusion" in the minds of characters and readers alike. This passage (pp. 117–23) is a brilliant exercise in critical improvisation and well worth the general price of admission.

Otherwise, except as a commemorative gesture, the book as a whole is a trifle disappointing. It is at once generous-minded and rather lazy and unventuresome. Warren's reading for it does not seem to have gone much beyond the main run of Dreiser's novels and some recent academic studies (notably those by Ellen Moers and Richard Lehan, both duly acknowledged). His rating of the novels follows the conventional wisdom. He sensibly passes over The "Genius", simply noting its crippling investment in "self-glorification," and draws by the way a useful distinction between the novels like Sister Carrie and Jennie Gerhardt that were written "out of [Dreiser's] life, but not about his life" and those that directly project his "dream-self," that woman-conquering, world-subduing superman who executed fantasies of revenge on a world, a society and destiny, that had made him an outsider from birth. This distinction would have been worth testing on less familiar material. An equally attentive reading of the memorial sketches in Twelve Men and the sizeable body of stories collected in Free and Chains would not only have confirmed it but would have given a fuller and truer picture of Dreiser's storytelling mastery. For it is a further paradox that this novelist who is a byword for grand-scale artistic clumsiness is nevertheless capable of an exemplary economy and concentration in shorter forms. His best sketches and tales are performatively as efficient as those of, say, Scott Fitzgerald—another unexpected admirer, who drew no small part of the elegiac rhapsody that closes The Great Gatsby from the final paragraphs of "W. L. S." in Twelve Men—and they match the novels as divinations of the form and pressure of actual life. And Robert Penn Warren, an erratic and oddly unpersuasive novelist but a superb natural raconteur, could have been just the man to open up this relatively disregarded sector of Dreiser's work for fresh examination.

With An American Tragedy the whole pattern of Dreiser's life—from the resentments and constraints of his irksome marriage and of every other private relationship we know anything about to the fatality that seemed to him to govern his own experience of success and failure in the world—is offered as the determining matrix. Warren's account of the book's long gestation and the blocking out of its essential story several years earlier in the autobiographies that became A Book About Myself and Dawn is skillful and convincing. As for his critical reading of the finished novel, it seems to me rather more than generous. Awkwardnesses of organization are noted in passing, but the claims advanced in Dreiser's title to the force and grandeur of genuine tragedy are accepted pretty much at face value, and the novel is granted an exemplary power to "involve" and "entrap" its readers. It draws forth "our own secret sense of doom," so that we "live into" Clyde Griffith's story and are implicated in it with him. The same profound involvement in the destiny and consciousness of the hero is assumed to be the case with the first two Cowperwood novels, The Financier and The Titan; again, Warren asserts that through the subtle dynamics of the advancing narration "we" are compelled "literally as well as figuratively" to act out Cowperwood's fate.

The interesting thing here, beneath these depressing *Saturday Review* banalities of critical commendation, is the support it gives to a sense Warren's whole book arouses of the resemblances between his own program as a novelist and the one he defines for Dreiser. In fact, the more he writes about the deep themes of *An American Tragedy*—personal identity and the illusoriness of conscious being; the "mulch of chemistry" underlying the desperate "drama of self-definition"—and about the character of Cowperwood and the inner workings of his drive to power, the closer we move to the world of *All the King's Men* and its progressively less captivating successors. In extracting from the Cowperwood novels definitions of an "ultimate wisdom" of life and, as a corollary, an "ultimate virtue" possible to men, and making these definitions a first measure of Dreiser's achievement, Warren chiefly reminds us of the fascination with Big Ideas that has marred his own major effort in fiction, pumping in philosophical rhetoric to do the work of first-order story-finding and story-telling. Jack Burden's "Big Twitch," which is given to us charged with Warren's own ruminative conviction, is only colloquially different from Dreiser's "chemisms" as an instrument of explanation and understanding. Take away that artist's grasp of the deep rhythms of life and consciousness which Warren handsomely identifies in Dreiser, and a depressing factitiousness of design remains that, in Warren's own fiction, no amount of anecdotal and mimetic skill can overcome.

Homage to Theodore Dreiser opens with three commemorative poems. The first two, offering a psychological and a sociological "profile," are in that equally factitious mode of language-bullying and psychologically reductive cracker-barrel hyperbole that disfigures all too much of Warren's effort in poetry; a mode in which it seems to make a great moral difference that aspirants to dignity and honor in human life are in plain truth "chinless wonders" with "potato-noses" who practice filthy secret vices like masturbation and nail-biting, and in which poetic credit is thought to accrue by the forthright use, at regular intervals, of tough words like "gut," "shank," "crotch," "ass," "cunt," "spit," "drool," "stink," "tumor," and "foetus"— all of which tells you what the human condition really is when you get down beneath all those high-minded pretensions. The third of these poems, called "Moral Assessment," is much more restrained and expressively modest. It seems to me a fine poem, truthful and technically accomplished, and

to compensate for some of the sourness of the foregoing comment it deserves
to be quoted whole:

> No psychiatrist need be called
> To anatomize his pain.
> He suffers but the kind all men
> Suffer in their human kind.
> No—suffers, too,
> His nobility of mind.
>
> He denies it, he sneers at it,
> In his icy nightmare of
> The superlative self;
> And tries, but cannot theorize past
> The knowledge that
> Others suffer, too, at last.
>
> He is no philosopher.
> His only gift is to enact
> All that his deepest self abhors,
> And learn, in his self-contemplating distress,
> The secret worth
> Of all our human worthlessness.

8

"The Flight of the Rocket" and "The Last Good Country"

Fitzgerald and Hemingway in the 1920s, and After

The upper Middle West of the United States, Fitzgerald's and Hemingway's home territory, is the hardest of American regions to characterize culturally and historically, though it is conceivably the easiest to be surprised by. During these writers' early lives it had been substantially settled and occupied for barely two generations. As a developed English-speaking society it was not older than Texas or California, and as American industrialization rolled forward in the later nineteenth century it was, if anything, more volatile, more continuously self-transforming. French-built St. Louis apart, the chief midwestern cities had been, as late as 1850, not much more than accidental commercial villages and frontier trading posts. In the decades following they had come to dominate the productive economy of the country and coincidentally to nurture, in their booming entrepreneurial expansion, a main share of post–Civil War popular mythology. The inventors Edison and Kettering were midwesterners, as were the illustrious generals who had salvaged victory in the war and, after 1869, most of the presidents who were absentmindedly overseeing America's surge to world power and influence. So too, by birth or adoption, were Rockefeller and McCormick, Henry Ford and Clement Studebaker (model for Dreiser's Archibald Kane), Orville and Wilbur Wright and the founders—Armour, Swift—of Chicago's meatpacking fortunes, and, equal to any, the indisputably fabulous James J. Hill, who, coming at eighteen to 1850s St. Paul (five years later than Fitzgerald's embarrassingly self-made and Irish-born grandfather), built the St. Paul Pacific and Great Northern railroads and in alliance with the New Yorker J. P. Morgan outgeneraled E. H. Harriman himself in the gigantic merger battles of 1901.

At all levels men of this era built their lives in the upper Middle West on the jagged cusp between the original frontier and runaway modernization. Like Hemingway's doctor-father, they might settle into professional practice in a prosperous new Chicago suburb, supporting in comfort wives and children anxious for both social rank and individual notice of some undefined sort, and yet return as often as they could to the ruggedness of frontier conditions, as to the near wilderness of northern Michigan, where as a boy Hemingway discovered his lifelong passion for shooting and fishing and the tactical mastery of difficult terrain.

Far more than in later decades the chief midwestern cities during this expansive half-century also took the lead in cultural innovation. Not only its geographically central location mandated the choice of Chicago as site of the World's Columbian Exposition of 1893. It was from a base in Chicago that the economist Veblen mockingly dissected the twin systems of modern business enterprise and modern leisure-class self-gratification; it was in Chicago that Louis Sullivan and Frank Lloyd Wright set about revolutionizing American architectural practice. It was in newspaper offices in Chicago and other midwestern cities that Dreiser gained his earliest national reputation, as did, after him, the mordantly innovative vernacular satirists George Ade and Ring Lardner. And it was in Chicago first of all that American literary modernism began to stabilize its voice and outlook, with the founding of Harriet Monroe's *Poetry* in 1912 and Margaret Anderson's *Little Review* in 1913. More or less inevitably it was to Chicago that the autodidact midwestern modernist Sherwood Anderson, who published in both journals and would leave his narrative stamp on early stories of both Hemingway (1898–1961) and Fitzgerald (1896–1940), came to begin re-creating himself as an autochthonous American artist.

In the Midwest after 1900 the rules for art as for the whole conduct of life were there to be remade. An American from the Midwest—in a detail of popular mythology picked up by the East Coast narrator of Edmund Wilson's *I Thought of Daisy* (1929)—"might turn into anything." So he might, at twenty-five, brashly set about competing as an equal with the recognized masters of his trade and begin at once, as Fitzgerald wrote Max Perkins in 1922, to create in his own fashion "something *new*—something extraordinary and beautiful and simple and intricately patterned." At the same time the midwestern temper was, rather to its own chagrin, self-consciously provincial, looking east and to Europe for ultimate approval. Confident of being at "the warm center of the world"—the words are Nick Carraway's in *The Great Gatsby*—it was also wary of being exposed, especially following its excited excursion eastward into the Great War, as only at "the ragged edge" of a newly formed and still forming cultural universe. It was securely planted yet indefinably restless and unsettled, producing after 1910 and 1920 both the monumental complacency that made *Main Street* and *Babbitt* period bywords and young ambitions ready to capitalize without constraint on a new era's superflux of fresh creative opportunity.

For Fitzgerald and Hemingway as writers, the particular form of opportunity was determined by the onrush of Anglo-European modernism, that liberation of individual talent in all the arts in which Americans like Eliot, Pound, and Gertrude Stein were already formative influences. It was the modernist renaissance, and the new openness of judgment and behavior generally, that drew them as writers to Paris in the early 1920s, as it was the emergent critical consensus supporting modernism that, greeting with discriminating approval what they themselves considered their best work, helped each establish an authorial identity he could not subsequently live down, an identity that as time went on became both challenge and burden. Inevitably they met in Paris in the mid-twenties; living and working only in the United States, they might well not have done so. From that point forward their careers and reputations closely shadowed each other, not least in their own competitive self-scrutiny. Sharp differences in temperament, in popularity and fortune, and of course in compositional signature only heighten for us, half a century later, impressions of a fundamental resemblance.

Each of them, for example, came early and all at once into his distinctive mastery. (It was the period, Gertrude Stein later remarked, when "everybody was twenty-six.") Each accomplished, before reaching thirty, work he would not afterward surpass or even quite match, except fragmentarily. Each achieved that limited yet intense originality of style which sooner or later attracts bluff parody but which no one else can betray into parody as they themselves did—styles capable of single passages as poignant and memorable as great lyric poetry, startling readers into recognition of things massively felt but not yet distilled into precise awareness. Each of them, too, it may finally be said, found one central story to tell and one story only, establishing it early and returning to it again and again. Each strikes us, even at his best, as writing from a condition of intense imaginative arrest, a condition that nevertheless furnishes an attentive steadiness and conviction able at times to counterfeit the most complex imaginative control. Each seems to have carried forward from the beginning a burden of self-doubt that returns again and again as a directing theme; so each regularly projects, in his most durable work, morally compromised narrators who are a few important years older than the writer himself at the time of writing and who become, at critical points in the story, party to the worst corruption narrationally on offer.

Each, that is, spoke through a narrating voice of a certain fixed kind, one looking back without relief to some catastrophic turning point that cannot be reversed or, concurrently, to some lost and mourned alternative. Fitzgerald mainly elects to give us the flash and wide flare that forerun the predestined catastrophe. He gives us, to use his own figure, the upward "flight of the rocket"—provisional title for *The Beautiful and Damned*, his first fully calculated major undertaking. Hemingway pivots his relentless narratives of disaster and defeat around ironic recollections of lost primal circumstance, symbolized in particular by the vision of some "last good country"—title of the latest and longest of his autobiographic Nick Adams stories. But the cohering fictional and interpretive logic driving each man's story forward seems much the same, born from the same explosive convergence of historical occasion and native circumstance.

2

Fitzgerald, three years senior, was sooner off the mark. Exposed at an eastern school and at Princeton to at least headline notions of modern literary seriousness and favored by the attention of a few extraordinary undergraduate friends (Edmund Wilson and John Peale Bishop first of all), he aimed high from the start, if only in transferring reveries of being one of "the big men" of his time from the context of college athletics and student theatricals to that of high literary achievement. When at twenty-one he began constructing a novel his head was overrun with competing models of up-to-date excellence. This project's original title was *The Romantic Egotist*, a pairing of lecture-hall categorizations that suggests the particular character of its normal enough first-novel factitiousness. It may also suggest something essential to genuineness of achievement at any level: a sense on the one hand, however limited its first expression, of what affective focus gives the greatest authenticity to the writer's central intuitions, and on the other, in that first title's loosely oxymoronic form, of the need to balance self-projection with undeceived self-judgment. At the core of all Fitzgerald's writing is a surprisingly resourceful intuition of the logistics as well as the pathos of modern egoism, the glamor to itself but equally the self-destructiveness. But his very soundness of conception on this ground too often allowed him to be careless and uncertain in devising a structure for what he knew to say.

In purpose and design *This Side of Paradise* (1920) spills all over the place, though it has the beguiling impudence to try to make aesthetic capital of its own disorderliness. Its remarkable public success assured Fitzgerald that he was on a composite track worth following. An exercise in a displaced bourgeois-suburban version of the coming-of-age format that in English fiction traces back through Compton Mackenzie's *Sinister Street* to *The Ordeal of Richard Feverel*, *This Side of Paradise* aims at being as well a frontline history of contemporary morals and of an epoch-marking revolution in popular manners. It also aims at assessing the uncharted social and historical transformations that furnish its episodic matrix. The transparently autobiographical protagonist is someone who, as we hear in the last chapter's Shavian dialogue with a "big man" from the world of corporate power, has read Walter Lippmann on drift and mastery and Henry Adams on modern historical acceleration as well as Shaw himself; the theme-codifying prefaces to Shaw's plays are an obvious model for the division into short titled sections that ratchets the story forward and covers for its shortfall of dramatic consequence.

Shaw's epigrammatic conciseness and the hyperbolic American equivalent to be found circa 1920 in H. L. Mencken's commentaries were valuable antidotes to *Sinister Street*, a doubly bad precedent with its 800-plus pages about youthful self-centeredness facing a compromised world and its Edwardian mix of neo-Gothic sensationalism and modern disenchantment ("a voice insinuating, softly metallic . . . fingers that touched his wrist as lightly as silk . . . a horrible sense of publicity . . . of money hard and round and powerful"). But Fitzgerald—that one among the younger writers, Gertrude Stein said, "who wrote naturally in sentences"—trusted too much to phrase-making, to the forced adjective, the offhand analytic generalization, the snap of a moralizing summary. What is intended as shrewdly penetrating comes off as mere knowingness ("She had that curious mixture of the social and artistic temperaments found often in two classes, society women and actresses"). To any reader for whom, after *The Great Gatsby*, Long Island will forever be "that slender riotous island which extends itself due east from New York," the sprinkling of words like "riotous" all around the early fiction—the Princeton Triangle show as "a riotous mystery" and so forth— is a performative embarrassment.

Fitzgerald's overdrawn second novel, *The Beautiful and Damned* (1922), was even more of a patch-up, yet stands as a more ambitious attempt at full-dress psychological portraiture and at a representative chapter of contemporary moral history. Neither the title nor the airy knowingness of the opening sentence—"In 1913, when Anthony Patch was twenty-five, two years were already gone since irony, the Holy Ghost of this later day, had, theoretically at least, descended upon him"—are encouraging portents. But in charting the marriage and life-progress of two children of American wealth reared to take unquestioningly for their own all that pleased them in life and seeking in every crisis only to be "comfortable and safe" in some recovered simulacrum of childhood protectedness, the novel takes on more affective momentum than, on any page, its self-preening swagger would seem to permit. It has the ambiguous pressure of Fitzgerald's own moral vanity behind it, source of both his worst lapses and his truest apprehensions. (It has also his rising ambivalence about his own hectically glamorous marriage and career.) In its basically simple design the book bears an odd resemblance to Dreiser's powerful *Sister Carrie* (1900), most of all when the draining away of the male protagonist's moral strength is set against the still-ascending curve of the "almost masculine" heroine's self-possession, though in the end she does not succeed as an actress and he regresses into infantilism and the company of Ivy League dullards and wastrels. It may be seen as a version of *Sister Carrie* (whose author Fitzgerald as of 1924 considered, along with Mencken, "the most important man in the country") composed by someone who has found out about Flaubert's *Sentimental Education*. It is also, in clear outline, a mock-up of *Tender Is the Night*, Fitzgerald's short-circuited masterwork of the 1930s.

Interestingly this novel's best moments are perhaps its most surrealistic, when Fitzgerald's trademark blend of excitability and apprehensiveness precipitates directly in something random and phantasmagoric—like the moment on the eve of Anthony Patch's marriage when the noise of a woman's demented laughter comes to him across an alleyway as the noise of life itself: "Life was that sound out there, that ghastly reiterated female sound." It is possible to think that the best of the stories Fitzgerald was pouring out and successfully marketing alongside his first two novels are those most open to the same fantastication.

These early stories, one after another set out along some pattern of vaulting hopefulness and remorseless disillusion, have been praised for their social acuity, their control over the complex stratifications of American behavior. But the farther in time we stand from them, the more narrowly angled seems their grasp on any actual society. This is not simply a matter of their absorption in the rituals of wealth and near-wealth. What they know, what Fitzgerald himself knew, is an affective reality independent of the particulars of actual social encounter but also possibly—and this is its strength—anterior to them: the reality, that is, of socially expressed envy and humiliation, of unappeasable restlessness and raw unfocused desiring. Over and over these stories tell how, faced with everything unanticipatable in modern life, the imagination takes refuge in alternating fantasies of domination and ruin, magical conquest and equally magical, or demonic, frustration and bafflement.

In plotting his stories Fitzgerald depended on contrivances and interventions as manipulative as those patented by O. Henry, still the master spirit of the popular magazine market. As good a later story as "Babylon Revisited," with its compounded representation of loss and regret and ambiguous self-accounting, pivots on a single arbitrary shock of accidental intrusion. Not even "Absolution," prospecting the ground from which a year later Fitzgerald would draw forth the history of Jay Gatsby, escapes a sense of narrative forcing. Only when the matter of the story becomes at every turn a function of the consciousness of the central agent, making the general dream-vision his dream, does it effectively overcome—and "Winter Dreams" is as good an instance as any—this hovering artificiality.

Or when the fantastication that underpins the whole comes directly to the surface and begins to compose the whole narrational circumstance. This further release into extravagance is what brings off a jokey entertainment like "Rags Martin-Jones and the Pr–nce of W–les." The major achievement of this kind is surely "The Diamond As Big as the Ritz" (1922). In this long story, virtually a novella, a superbuccaneering Gilded Age family named

Washington has built up over three generations a murderous, slave-holding fortress and pleasure palace on top of a diamond mountain and stands prepared in its "monstrous condescension" to fight off any threat from outside and to bring on general holocaust if other strategies fail. "The Diamond" qualifies, in its self-delighting preposterousness, as the ultimate America-as-Eldorado story; it stands solidly between Fenimore Cooper's prophetic allegory of the fortunes of the Republic in *The Crater* (1847) and the rocket-flight apocalypse of Pynchon's *Gravity's Rainbow* (1973). And more than anything Fitzgerald had yet published, it anticipates the extraordinary convergence of personal and national mythologizing that he famously achieved in *The Great Gatsby* (1925).

One other factor in the unlikely success of "The Diamond" is the split perspective gained by its presentation through the eyes of an outsider, a young man from some bypassed town in the American heartland. Indeed, as a final patch of dialogue hints, the entire fantasy may be its two young survivors' own mid-American dream. (" 'It *was* a dream,' said John quietly. 'Everybody's youth is a dream, a sort of chemical madness.' ") In *The Great Gatsby* the same split perspective is all-important. Gatsby's self-propelled rocket flight to grandeur and squalid oblivion provides the central coordinates for the narrative text itself, which enacts—in the first-person voice—Nick Carraway's double education into moral reality and into the contradictory covenants at the center of American history.

This simplest of compositional shifts, from third-person to first-person narration, proved both stabilizing and reempowering to Fitzgerald's repertory of performative tricks. It gives context to his insistent phrase-making; accepting Nick's throwaway ironies about the "usually plagiaristic" intimacies of young men or about wanting "no more riotous excursions with privileged glimpses into the human heart," we are, by the second page, ready to acquiesce in his claiming for his protagonist "a romantic readiness such as I have never found in any other person" and in his assurance that the cause of his own overpowering disillusionment is not anything Gatsby has been or done but what has preyed on Gatsby, "what foul dust floated in the wake of his dreams." The book's judgmental lines of force could not be more precisely drawn. Nick's interventions make a space, too, for the expert mimicry of a whole subordinate range of self-betraying American voices—Catherine Wilson's whispered "Neither of them can stand the person they're married to," the racketeer Wolfsheim's valedictory "such a mad act as that man did should make us all think," or a drunken party guest's confidential explanation of why he was so slow getting out of the car he has smashed into a ditch: "At first I din' notice we'd stopped." More important, the first-person refractions cover over, or nearly do, the parts of the story—Gatsby's actual business life or, as Fitzgerald wrote to Edmund Wilson, "the emotional relations between Gatsby and Daisy from the time of their reunion to the catastrophe"—that Fitzgerald admitted he had no clear feeling about and hadn't thought through. What he hadn't himself imagined thus merges convincingly enough with what Nick Carraway finds barely conceivable and responds to as mysterious, fantastic.

Above all, Nick's confessional narrative suffuses the improbabilities of Gatsby's history with the pathos and conviction of his own encounters with contemporary reality. A showcase instance would be the famous listing in Chapter IV of all those who came to Gatsby's parties the summer of the story, "gray names" on a "disintegrating" timetable which is nevertheless hardly two years old (a detail in that poetry of time that is one of the book's deftest achievements). A simpler one is the brief run of paragraphs in Chapter II laying out the novel's metropolitan theater of action, force-field for both its excitements and its conspiratorial exclusions:

> I began to like New York, the racy, adventurous feel of it at night, and the satisfactions that the constant flicker of men and women and machines gives to the restless eye. I liked to walk up Fifth Avenue and pick out romantic women from the crowd and imagine that in a few minutes I was going to enter into their lives, and no one would ever know or disapprove. . . . Again at eight o'clock, when the dark lanes of the Forties were lined five deep with throbbing taxicabs, bound for the theater district, I felt a sinking in my heart. Forms leaned together in the taxis as they waited, and voices sang, and there was laughter from unheard jokes, and lighted cigarettes made unintelligible circles inside.

The Great Gatsby is not flawless. Undergraduate smartiness pushes back in; the weak gag about Gatsby's identifying San Francisco as in the Middle West (to confirm the "something a little sinister" Nick senses in him?) is totally implausible, and the charged lines early in chapter VI defining the protagonist as "a son of God"—"a phrase which, if it means anything, means just that"—comes off as patchwork bluster. More than once the set of balancing acts the narrative advances by seems ready to topple. But all such shifts and dodges are eternally forgiven in the beauty and precision of the last pages, when the unloving Buchanans' "money or . . . vast carelessness, or whatever it was that kept them together" is set in place as the unyielding nemesis of the whole affair, and Gatsby's absurd dream recedes into "that vast obscurity beyond the city, where the dark fields of the republic rolled on under the night."[1]

The book's achievement, unequivocally praised by judges as authoritative as Edith Wharton and T. S. Eliot, haunted Fitzgerald. With *Tender Is the Night* (1934), much delayed and never structurally resolved, he returned in Book One (as originally printed) to a version of the narrative refraction used in *Gatsby*; but once his Hollywood starlet has performed her function in building up the elusive attractiveness of the main couple, she becomes only a plot device. The book stands as a more elegant and sustained reenactment of *The Beautiful and Damned* with, as it progresses, a corresponding attenuation. (Yet there is a fine recovery in the short last chapter, at least for readers knowing something of the forlorn geography of western New York State.) Some Fitzgerald partisans find evidence of a return to mastery in *The Last Tycoon*, posthumous and unfinished, but the ineffectiveness of filtering key impressions through the sensibility of a young woman infatuated with the movie-producer hero, and the triviality of studio episodes meant to display the hero's magnetism and romantic integrity, suggest otherwise. The "unassuming dignity" that Anthony Powell remembered about Fitzgerald's personal presence in 1930s Hollywood, and certainly the graciousness and good humor, register better in his abundant correspondence and in the personal, and confessional, essays Edmund Wilson collected after his death in *The Crack-Up*.

3

Fitzgerald's strongest work in the 1920s is built on a fundamental disproportion between the tawdry excitements and miseries of the given story and the vast moral and historical importance that in one way or another attaches to them. To his midwestern adaptability and the broad stimulus of modernism, the era of his coming of age added one other shaping influence: the sustained national self-audit occupying American writers and thinkers after 1917.[2]

---

1. A confirmation of Fitzgerald's attentive respect for Dreiser is his adaptation, in writing out Nick's visionary final musings, of the passage that closes the last sketch in *Twelve Men* (1919).

2. These were the years of *The Seven Arts* and *The Dial*, Mencken's *American Language*, Waldo Frank's *Our America*, Santayana's *Character and Opinion in the United States*, Van Wyck Brooks's diagnostic studies of Twain and James, Harold Stearns's symposium *Civilization in the United States*,

The same instinct for discovering in the marginal affairs of a few persons the temper and direction of a whole society and era enters into Hemingway's brilliantly precocious narratives from the start. With a first handful of laconic one- and two-paragraph sketches of scenes of war and the bull ring—sketches that became the numbered interchapters of In Our Time (1925)—Hemingway stepped directly, at twenty-four, into the company of Pound and Ford, Joyce and Gertrude Stein. After two novels and a second collection of stories he was, at thirty, chef d'école for a whole rising American and European generation in prose fiction. The force of his presence reached beyond the contagiousness of his remarkable style. "More than any other writer," V. S. Pritchett would write in 1941, "he has defined for us the personality of our own time."

His own formalized accounts of that style are not fully reliable as guides to its effectiveness. In the familiar passage at the beginning of Death in the Afternoon (1932) describing his early motives and purposes, the stress is on fidelity to primary emotion ("knowing what you really felt, rather than what you were supposed to feel, and had been taught to feel") and on unob-structed facticity ("what really happened in action; what the actual things were which produced the emotion that you experienced"). The passage in A Farewell to Arms (1929) at the beginning of the masterfully dramatized Caporetto debacle, about the obscenity of words like sacred, glorious, hallow, and in vain alongside "the concrete names of villages, the numbers of roads, the names of rivers, the numbers of regiments and the dates," bears the same minimalist emphasis. But the expert opening sentence of A Farewell is nothing if not abstract and generalized. "In the late summer of that year we lived in a house in a village that looked across the river and the plain to the mountains"—what in fact this immediately establishes are two literally spell-binding tonalities: an intimacy of address (that year, we lived) coercing us into becoming accomplices in the narrator's tensely precise act of valedictory recollection, and the constrained watchfulness or apprehen-siveness drawing observation out from house and village over a neutral space of river and plain—the prepositions and single conjunction taking on the propulsive force of verbs—to the foreboding mountains from which, sooner or later, the trouble is coming.

The power of that simple, paratactic style to project or recover felt experience overwhelmed its early hearers. Cyril Connolly, speaking as

Williams's In the American Grain, Hart Crane's The Bridge, and of mass-circulation scholarly works like Parrington's Main Currents in American Thought and the Beards' Rise of American Civilization.

"Palinurus," bears witness: "The greatness of Hemingway is that he alone of living writers has saturated his books with the memory of physical pleasure, with sunshine and salt water, with food, wine and making love, and with the remorse which is the shadow of that sun." But this, too, a little misrepresents the scope and solidity of observation in the early writing. It fits well enough the memorable set piece midway into *The Sun Also Rises* (1926) on the fishing trip into the hills beyond Burguete, through beech woods and shaded grass to cold, clear white-water streams—one more representation of the purged and restorative "good country" of Hemingway's repetitive mythmaking. It doesn't, however, do full justice to the calculated impact of quite casual descriptions, as of the car ride bringing Jake Barnes, the book's narrator, up from Bayonne toward the Spanish frontier, a passage lightly evoking the occupational integrity of a whole alternative society and so beginning to make firm the moral dynamic, between integrity and corruption, outflowing release and sterility, the main action of the novel will turn on:

> We passed some lovely gardens and had a good look back at the town, and then we were out in the country, green and rolling, and the road climbing all the time. We passed lots of Basques with oxen, or cattle, hauling carts along the road, and nice farmhouses, low roofs, and all white-plastered. In the Basque country the land all looks very rich and green and the houses and villages look well-off and clean. Every village had a pelota court and on some of them the kids were playing in the hot sun. There were signs on the walls of the churches saying it was forbidden to play pelota against them, and the houses in the villages had red tiled roofs, and then the road turned off and commenced to climb.

Green pastoral hills and travel-poster villages, to be sure, but also—carefully noted—flourishing gardens, well-kept houses and fields, men and animals at work; a society, in brief, with firm rules and customs, ceremonial institutions and licensed departures, that will prove capable as the full story develops of effectively resisting and assimilating foreign profanation.

The secret of these effects is not simply in the spare vocabulary and syntax—Hemingway, when he wanted to, could uncoil sentences as overloaded as Faulkner's—but in attaching what is registered to some active sequence of reimagined experience. Two early sentences in the nostalgia-drenched late memoir, A *Moveable Feast*, show how this narrative style works at its simplest and how easily it collapses into mannerism. In the book's first paragraph: "We would have to shut the windows in the night against the rain and the cold wind would strip the leaves from the trees in the Place Contrescarpe." "In the night," rather than "at night," shifts us from generalized summary to a particular remembered moment, and the action of the wind is what would in fact be observed from an about-to-be-shut window. In the first paragraph of the chapter following, the basic structure of statement is repeated and with an extra touch of explanatory concreteness—"We burned *boulets* which were molded, egg-shaped lumps of coal dust, on the wood fire, and on the streets the winter light was beautiful"—but without the jog of a specific remembered instance, the effect is willful and self-parodying. Interestingly, the difference matches an evident difference in the two recollections. The first is of an event that in however small a way was forced on the observing consciousness; the pleasurable impression is salvaged from something initially discomforting. The second is of circumstances calculatingly (and self-approvingly) created. Its very inconsequence calls attention to something intrusive in the passage: a determination first of all to establish credentials, to be known for fine taste—slightly esoteric but thoroughly naturalized—and discriminating sensory judgment. (The difference offers a micro-instance of the falsifications that overtook Hemingway's later writing and mar even as well managed a construct as *For Whom the Bell Tolls*, his most resolutely ambitious novel. When he built his narratives on the recollection of events and actions that he had had no choice not to undergo and absorb, that had come to him—like those of boyhood and young manhood—under their own impulsion, that peculiarly studious and attentive habit of mind which to Malcolm Cowley marked him off from the rest of the young expatriate talents in the mid-twenties could operate without interference. When later on, living more and more inside a self-fabricated personal myth, he began making books out of activities and places he had elected for the sake of the pleasure anticipated from them—Africa and the Caribbean, fishing and big-game hunting—there is a palpable loss of control.)

The famous style, with its projection of a corresponding ethic and a whole measured strategy for maintaining balance against the onslaughts of temporal experience, is nowhere more efficient than in passages of dialogue. Both the short stories and the novels depend heavily on dialogue: on otherwise unspecified shifts of tone between speakers, alternations of intimacy and formality, or on sudden silences—like the silence and then aggressive sharpness of speech overtaking the punched-up prizefighter in the beautifully accomplished early story, "The Battler." The dramatic range of this practice of dialogue is distinctly limited. With young women characters, most of all the protagonists' accommodating girlfriends, it is nearly always at the edge, or well over it, of factitiousness—though special honors are due the seven unbroken "please"s with which the pregnant girl in "Hills Like White Elephants" begs her caddish lover to "stop talking." But no one has ever done better at entering into the conspiracies of male comradeship; the solidity of secondary characterizations, like the army doctor Rinaldi in A Farewell to Arms and indeed of a dozen and more supernumerary soldiers, priests, hotel and customs and police personnel, is all in their overheard voices. Friends who knew Hemingway well remembered, according to Carlos Baker, a "special clairvoyance" in interpersonal contacts (along with an appalling gift for bullying); the American diplomat Ellis Briggs thought him the most perceptive man he had ever met in sensing nuances of interpersonal feeling. "In a group of people, if two of them were antagonistic to each other, Ernest felt it at once."

That atmosphere of antagonism, real or impending, is Hemingway's surest fictive invention, and it is made more intensely affecting by the dream of happiness and escape it breaks in upon. In all his writing, figures move between a world of violence where every life is at risk and the apprehension of another kind of world, one that is the purified image of their desiring. In The Sun Also Rises it is the fishing episode, and the austerity in general of Spanish manners and the Spanish landscape, that offset the grasping personal betrayals of the main story, the "[too] much wine . . . ignored tension, and . . . feeling of things coming that you could not prevent happening." In A Farewell to Arms the brief fantasy early in Book One about going up into the Abruzzi—"where the roads were frozen and hard as iron, where it was clear cold and dry and the snow was dry and powdery and hare-tracks in the snow and the peasants took off their hats and called you Lord and there was good hunting"—gives us an alternative world never quite lost sight of in the conflict and agony that follow.[3] In For Whom the Bell Tolls (1940) Spain itself, as realized in what Edmund Wilson accurately described as the "social romance" of the isolated guerrilla band, becomes the "good country" being ravaged and betrayed in the amoral violence of war. Even with the posthumous compilation, Islands in the Stream, where Hemingway's increasingly aggressive fears and fantasies run more and more out of control,

3. The power and shock of the ending of "The Snows of Kilimanjaro" (1936) spring, on the other hand, from our realization that the place "wide as all the world, great, high, and unbelievably white in the sun"—the snowy mountaintop itself—is the place of death.

that art of placing the action along some tense boundary between everything desirable and secure and something menacing in existence which can never be propitiated gives us one more precise and urgent opening description:

The house was built on the highest part of the narrow tongue of land between the harbor and the open sea. It had lasted through three hurricanes and it was built solid as a ship. It was shaded by tall coconut palms that were bent by the trade wind and on the ocean side you could walk out of the door and down the bluff across the white sand and into the Gulf Stream. The water of the Stream was usually a dark blue when you looked out at it when there was no wind. But when you walked out into it there was just the green light of the water over that floury white sand and you could see the shadow of any big fish a long time before he could ever come in close to the beach.

It was a safe and fine place to bathe in the day but it was no place to swim at night. At night the sharks came in close to the beach, hunting in the edge of the Stream, and from the upper porch of the house on quiet nights you could hear the splashing of the fish they hunted and if you went down to the beach you could see the phosphorescent wakes they made in the water. At night the sharks had no fear and everything else feared them. But in the day they stayed out away from the clear white sand and if they did come in you could see their shadows a long way away.

The body of Hemingway's writing is not large. Most of his novels have the concentration and compactness of novellas—even *For Whom the Bell Tolls*, as some first reviews recognized, may work best as a sequence of related stories—and the short stories he valued enough to keep in print make up, including the whole of *In Our Time*, a single volume. The range of behavioral observation is correspondingly narrow. Its strength and integrity at its best, however, remain undeniable, and almost invariably turn on some version of the dialectic of menace and escape, nightmarish violence and the dream of a sanctuary elsewhere. A final instance is that late addition to the Nick Adams cycle, written the year following the phenomenal popular (more than critical) success of *The Old Man and the Sea* (1952), which Hemingway provisionally titled "The Last Good Country." Here Nick, earlier seen as a small boy and then as a young man out of school and off to and back from the war, is the age of his great prototype, Huckleberry Finn, and is on the run from authority—game wardens out to punish him for out-of-season poaching. Not a little of the dialogue between Nick and his fiercely loyal kid sister (called "Littless"!) is in the late vein of stiff-lipped sentimentality, but as Nick goes on deeper into untracked woods and waters where no one has walked since Indian days, all that relish and precision in sizing up battle terrain that Hemingway's World War II associates reported of him come back into play, and the narrative gathers to itself once more the old excitement and conviction. It is another American tale of lighting out, *in extremis*, for "the territory," and as with Mark Twain, greatest of all mid-American fabulists, once Hemingway reached that point in it he could not imagine any sequel. The story, three times as long as even "Big Two-Hearted River," is one he never finished.

9

Pay Day

The Case of
Nathan Asch

In 1925 any knowledgeable listing of that new generation of American writers emerging to record the transformed sensibility of the post–World War I era—and in the process bring American fiction forward from provincial squeamishness into an unflinching modernity—would have included, along with Hemingway, Dos Passos, and Fitzgerald, the name of Nathan Asch. Asch, born in 1902, was the youngest of all these mid-1920s Paris-based expatriates, and like them he was promptly identified as a writer bent on confronting without evasions the revolutionized circumstance of everyday life in the megalopolitan twentieth century and on doing so through a corresponding modernization of style and narrative design. He came forward as one of Ford Madox Ford's avant-garde discoveries; during 1924 he had made three appearances in Ford's *transatlantic review*, in company with, among others, Hemingway, Dos Passos, Jean Rhys, Gertrude Stein, and the artists Brancusi and Picasso.

For this whole precocious group the year 1925 was indubitably an *annus mirabilis*. There was Hemingway's ambitiously titled *In Our Time*, Fitzgerald's *The Great Gatsby* ("the first step that American fiction has taken," T. S. Eliot assured its author, "since Henry James"), Dos Passos's *Manhattan Transfer*, marking completion of that young author's creative apprenticeship—and with them Nathan Asch's first novel, *The Office*, an episodic montage of scenes and private histories surveying the personnel of a Manhattan brokerage firm on the day of its collapse into bankruptcy. Asch's early prominence was solidified when one chapter of *The Office*, the self-contained story, "Gertrude Donovan," was selected for Edward J. O'Brien's influential anthology, *Best Short Stories of 1925*, alongside new work by Sherwood Anderson, Ring Lardner, Evelyn Scott, Glenway Wescott, and Elinor Wylie. (This was the annual collection that two years before had broadcast news of Hemingway's overnight emergence, at twenty-four, as a prose artist of indisputable consequence.)

The idea that no literary voice worth hearing will be wholly lost to future times is a consoling one, especially for writers whose careers after fine beginnings have unaccountably slowed down or vanished from general notice. Nathan Asch's life as a writer, it may be said, constitutes one of the notable failed careers in modern American letters. Before he was thirty he had published three novels, as many as Hemingway and Fitzgerald at the same age; the first and third of these, *The Office* (1925) and *Pay Day* (1930), were devoted specifically to the representation of contemporary city life at its most treacherous and corrupting, and they had enjoyed a success in translation, in Germany and Russia, that went well beyond their reasonably encouraging critical reception at home. Through the 1930s stories and articles by Asch appeared at intervals in *The New Yorker* and *The New Republic*, and he continued to hold the attention of major publishers. His 1935 chronicle of rural poverty and its victims' queer countermeasures, *The Valley* (set in the rundown district around Patterson, New York, where Asch, and the poets Allen Tate and Hart Crane, had occupied a farmhouse during the later 1920s), bore the respected Macmillan imprint. In 1937 W. W. Norton brought out, under the title *The Road: In Search of America*, his narrative of a journey of inquiry and observation to the West Coast and back through a country still mired in the Great Depression.

But *The Road*, appearing when he was only thirty-five, was to be Nathan Asch's last published book. After fair success as a Hollywood scriptwriter, a stint later in the 1930s at the Works Progress Administration's Washington headquarters, and wartime service with the Army Air Force at desk jobs in London and Paris, he returned to writing fiction and projected an ambitious sequence of novels meant to record the essential character of twentieth-century experience as it impinges on a representative modern and cosmo-politan sensibility. Apart from a scattering of magazine pieces, none of this work ever reached print. After 1940 the market for Asch's writing effectively vanished. Only Malcolm Cowley, that literary generation's most devoted historian, in sporadic footnotes and asides seemed to remember that Asch had existed and, despite disappointments, had never stopped working. In 1933 Granville Hicks's politically leftist study of modern American litera-ture, *The Great Tradition*, had treated him with respect as one of the more thoroughgoing of contemporary experimenters and as a predecessor of Dos Passos in the mode of the "collective novel." In John Hutchens's "literary panorama," *The American Twenties* (1952), and in Frederic J. Hoffman's overview, *The Twenties* (1965), Asch's name does not appear.

But in two vital respects Nathan Asch was from the start an odd fish in the post-1920 upsurge of new literary talent. In the first place he was not a birthright American. Born in Poland and brought into Western Europe before he was three, he had lived at intervals, until the first winter of World War I, in Germany and France as well as at Lodz in Poland (attending a Catholic school) and, during summers, in the Polish countryside, and he had spent his last pre-adolescent years in Paris, where his family—suspected of revolutionary sympathies in a still subjugated and partitioned Poland—had emigrated in 1912. Not until 1915 did he set foot in the United States, living first in Greenwich Village and then in a rural section of Staten Island. Near the end of his life Asch's memories of that first Paris interlude had grown dim, and he doubted that he had then learned very much about the city; but when he returned to Paris in the 1920s he was one of the few Americans whose fluency in French was not restricted to conversing with waiters and hotel managers.

Second, in becoming a writer Asch was not—in the manner set forth in Cowley's 1920s chronicle, *Exile's Return*—breaking ranks with the standard middle-American professional or business-class background, nor was he uprooting himself from the kind of provincial culture and locale that would remain the rich matrix for a Hemingway's, a Fitzgerald's, a Faulkner's storytelling. Instead he was moving directly in his own father's footsteps. By 1920 Sholem Asch (1880–1957) was internationally famous as a novelist and dramatist and, within his immediate cultural community, was venerated as a teacher and sage. For Polish students in the last years before World War I, Sholem Asch had been, as his son remembered long after, "a symbol of freedom." His stories and plays, written in Yiddish and grounded in the outlook and heritage of the Jewish *shtetl*, had been translated or performed throughout Europe and America; in 1924, the year of the son's maiden appearance in *transatlantic review*, an eighteen-volume edition of the father's writings was published in Warsaw. In the United States, where he was naturalized in 1920, Sholem Asch moved at once to the forefront of Jewish-American literary affairs. His fiction was serialized in the Yiddish press before being translated into English, and a weekly article he forced himself to write for papers like the *Daily Forward* (to make up for lost European royalties) became, as his son recalled, "that week's sermon for the Yiddish-speaking Jews of New York. When he walked along the streets of the Lower East Side, his name was whispered among the people with a kind of awe."

The burdens of being not only the eldest son of such a father but also an incipient professional rival may well be imagined. Near the end of his own life Nathan Asch wrote a long memoir of his father; its fair-mindedness and the over-all generosity of its judgments are much to the son's credit. Even in the abridged form in which it appeared, posthumously, in *Commentary* (January 1965), it sheds more than a little light on the altogether different trajectory of Nathan Asch's career. In it he remembers his father's evident satisfaction at his first printed effort, a book review for *The Nation*. Yet he also makes clear the near-complete absence of any common ground of literary understanding. From the beginning the differences in their creative equipment as well as in their public fortunes stood between them as a sign of professional, not to say filial, deviation and error. Two particular responses to his own advancing work are recorded in the memoir, without noticeable bitterness. " 'Speaking now as a writer,' my father had said on one occasion when I read him two stories I had written, 'I find no talent in you.' " And— in answer to a journalist's question when his son's stories had gained attention in Germany—" 'I have no opinion of him as a writer, but I still have to send him money.' " ("The wit is typical of him," Nathan Asch tonelessly comments.)

The radical differences between the two Asches' writings, and indeed between their basic outlook on life and experience, offer an exemplary contrast between two fundamental modes of literary effectiveness: the conventionalized and broadly popular, and avant-garde innovation and experiment. What comes across to any reader of the father's fluent and abundant work is what comes through with, on the whole, a forgiving clarity in the son's portrait: an intensity of self-absorption and a simple belief in the reality of his own fictional world that gave "vigor and breadth" (Malcolm Cowley's offhand description) to all his undertakings. The most flagrantly formulaic of Sholem Asch's stories somehow acquired, in the telling, a flavor of authenticity. Whether telling tales of *shtetl* life, or dramatizing in the trilogy *Three Cities* (1933) the epic human struggles of the Great War and the Russian Revolution, or re-creating in a context of Jewish history and tradition the lives of Jesus, Saint Paul, and the Virgin Mother—*The Nazarene* (1939), *The Apostle* (1943), *Mary* (1949)—Sholem Asch's fiction was a fairy-tale fiction in which, for all its naturalistic detail, simple parables of ideal virtue and villainy, beauty and wretchedness, generosity and self-serving, work themselves along to some stirring outcome. Correspondingly it was a fiction of fortuitous coincidences, chiaroscuro oppositions, pathetic (but predictable) reversals, set-piece digressions into the picturesque and the humanly representative, all of it interrupted at key moments by disquisitions on the typicality of what had just taken place and the particular truth or wisdom thus revealed. But it was also a fiction rooted in folk-consciousness and folk-sentiment—hence its broad popularity—and it was driven by a storytelling imagination that seems comfortably innocent of any other way of representing human existence. It thus derived from working methods and motives diametrically opposite to those Nathan Asch remembered setting out with in the modernist 1920s: "the rigid determination with which I faced my writing, the undeviating truth that I tried to get down."

This was to be first of all a truth about immediate interpersonal sensations and responses. In his memoir Nathan Asch recalls a final argument with his father concerning the nature and uses of good fiction. "He said that it would be impossible to tell the truth about the relation between people, while I maintained that it was possible, and that I would try to do it." But Nathan Asch's stubborn allegiance to a spare, precise truthfulness came to him more by default than by calculated choice. A detail that stays in mind from the memoir of his father is that he himself, though also native to Jewish Poland, never learned to speak or read his parents' first language. As a consequence, he lacked direct contact with the richness of folk tradition always available to his father. He had instead, within an adopted literary language, only a lyric factuality to fall back on for narrative effect. Malcolm Cowley granted that Nathan Asch could write "more lyrically" than his famous father and "with deeper feeling." What he lacked was the confident power to develop a compelling central story, with its narrational seaswell of crisis and climax;

a power that Sholem Asch could replenish at need from the vast storehouses of Yiddish storytelling and legend-making. A publisher's reader for the first of the son's post–World War II novel sequence, "Paris Is Home" (completed in 1947), praised its tactile descriptions of liberated Paris and its observant rendering of postwar attitudes but noted that it had no real narrative structure, no commanding story. More than minor revisions were needed; there would have to be "a new series of climactic episodes." But this was precisely what Nathan Asch could not provide, despite a continuing show of interest among editors and agents. He spoke to friends about revisions in progress, but the surviving manuscript shows virtually no sign of any.

In his early writing Nathan Asch shared that preoccupation with the lives of the insulted and injured, the victims of modern life, that dates back in modern American fiction to the work of Stephen Crane and Theodore Dreiser in the 1890s and early 1900s. Strictly speaking, the main character-izations in *The Office*, *Pay Day*, and *The Valley* are not of the proletariat or industrial working class. Two or three failed executives apart, the personnel of *The Office* are men and women of the white-collar crowd; despite every sort of anxiety and discouragement they are, in their own eyes, still upwardly mobile. They are junior clerks, administrative secretaries, division manag-ers, and—among the men—disaffected middle-class husbands and sons. They are dangling men (Saul Bellow's title phrase, twenty years later); men bedeviled by the ethos of material success who inwardly, however, have really "never wanted much" (foreshadowing Sloan Wilson's gray-flannel dissident of the 1950s). Living in essential isolation, they have got stuck inside the prevailing societal regimen and have never found out what it might mean to take control of their own lives. The lumpen-bourgeois hero of *Pay Day* is a figure from the same broad class, in hopeless spiritual flight from a dead-end office job and a household of peevish, disappointed women.

So it is a final irony in Nathan Asch's relation to his best-selling father that for all his insistence on undeviating truthfulness and an ultimate accuracy in representing human relationships, he never approached Sholem Asch's palpable success in rendering the rich textures of popular life—the ordinary predicaments, the countervailing resources, the confused yet irre-pressible communalism and hopefulness among the working masses, in particular those of New York's ethnically fragmented immigrant population. Sholem Asch's 1946 novel *East River*, spanning roughly a generation in the history of a single block of Jews, Slavs, Italians, and Irish on Manhattan's East Side, is as formulaic as a Frank Capra movie script. But it mixes conventionalized melodrama and a narrative style as garrulous and wisdom-avid as Thomas Wolfe's with much shrewd factual observation of the ways of life, honorable or crooked, its polyglot characters have salvaged from diminished or broken circumstance. It also makes an engaging show of planting its long narrative daydream in commonly remembered history. The cheerful arrival of "Alexander's Ragtime Band" on New York's summer sidewalks and, later, the hypnotic incursions of Harlem jazz (its "jungle motifs" allegedly stirring atavistic lusts and undermining the precious stabilities of family life) are duly recorded, along with the eager socialist propagandizing of pre-1917 "radicals" and the New York financial establishment's consequent hysteria about "revolution" and "anarchy." In particular, there is a detailed tabulation of the dreadful labor conditions bringing proposals for unionization and reform into the helter-skelter garment industry: disease-breeding sweatshops, the brutal exploitation of children and young women, and at the same time the pathetic complicity of working people themselves in circumventing the reformers for the sake of their meager, desperately pieced-out earnings. As Nathan Asch fifteen years earlier had made use of the epoch-marking Sacco-Vanzetti case to set off the main action of *Pay Day*, Sholem Asch in *East River* brought his story to an early climax in the holocaust of the 1911 Triangle Company fire, a decisive actual event in the rise of the powerful International Ladies Garment Workers Union.[1]

In the artful compound it makes of folk romance, liberal sentiment, and popularized recent history, *East River* was a solid commercial success, though not on the scale of Sholem Asch's Biblical epics; it was these grand and, for Sholem Asch's Jewish following, scandalously syncretic re-creations of New and Old Testament myth that every three or four years through the 1940s and 1950s brought his name to the top of the best-seller lists. There is indeed, in the literary fortunes of the two Asches, a curious reversal of the classic patterns of American immigrant experience. Supposedly it is the second generation in immigrant families that becomes Americanized and learns to interpret an alien world to its bewildered elders. But although (according to Nathan Asch's memoir) his father never learned to write in English, he had no difficulty in making contact with his mass American readership. He knew what the reading public wanted. (In *East River* he went so far, just two years before the establishment of the state of Israel, as to

1. Even a still young and hale New York State legislator named Franklin Roosevelt makes a cameo appearance in *East River*; he is shown entering sympathetically into conversation with a fervent East Side reformer who has fought back from crippling paralysis to lead the fight for workplace justice. Never one to miss a good opening, Sholem Asch gives young Roosevelt a speech expressing surprise that grown men as well as small children can be struck down by infantile paralysis.

give his young Jewish reformer a set speech in praise of America as the Jewish people's true homeland, where the social idealism of Jefferson, Lincoln, Wilson, and the Roosevelts would provide the place of fulfillment for the messianic hopes of the prophets.) It was instead the son who never "assimilated"—no more than he could conceive, in his novels, of steering the narrative toward those ultimate convergences of warm fellow feeling that after much suffering regularly brought his father's storytelling to some spirit-lifting conclusion.

Nathan Asch was ruefully aware of, by contrast, his own cultural detach-ment and disaffection. To Malcolm Cowley, in January 1931, he gave this account of what he felt to be his essential placelessness:

> I am not American, and probably if I never went back to Europe and lost all contact with it, and remained in America I still would never be an American. . . . But the curious thing is that I love this place and feel no sympathy with Eastern Europe. . . . So you see I have no place anywhere. . . . I love America, and am not American, not liked by Americans.

When, following publication of The Valley, he applied in 1936 for a Guggenheim Fellowship (he was turned down), his proposal statement became a testament to the understanding he had formed of his own situation as a writer and as a historical personage:

> The problem to be examined is one of rootlessness. Most writers, like most persons, have within them the memory of a home— physical: they spent their childhood in one house, went to one school, grew up, played, fought in one neighborhood—a spiritual home: they relax in one language, one region, one country. They are motivated by its tabus, are moved by love for it, are loyal to it. . . . their past flows in an unbroken line into their present, sustains and explains it. There seems to be, there seems always to have been, a quality to being native. It is a quality the writer of this statement does not possess.

The condition defined is the master theme of all Asch's writing. So the over-all title of his post-1945 novel sequence was to be "marginal Man": "the story," as he summed it up, "of forty years in the life of a Jew from Eastern Europe in the West." (Besides "Paris Is Home," only one other novel in this sequence, "London Is a Lonely Town," was completed; neither was published.) But it was in a novel he had already written, in which he had managed for once to fit every part of what he had to say into a single dramatized episode, that he best realized his undeniable gift for graphically precise description and his ideal of an unguarded candor and truthfulness. That novel was *Pay Day*. More immediately shocking in its matter-of-factness about sexuality than Asch's other published work, it was issued by a relatively obscure firm, Brewer and Warren, in February 1930, four months into the Depression. It bore the simple dedication, "For My Father."

2

By the end of *Pay Day* the book's curt title has taken on a multiple resonance. The first chapter places us at the close of the workweek's final day, with the featureless protagonist—his full name, Jim Cowan, is not given until we are twenty pages into the novel—hurrying away from his clerk's job in a business office and counting out his miserable weekly earnings. His immediate concern is with how much will be left, after paying off petty debts and surrendering a share to his mother for household expenses, to spend on himself and on a lunchroom waitress whose breasts he has been ogling and whom he has finally managed to make a date with for the evening ahead. He has got what is owed him for a week's work. But well before the story ends we see that he is being paid off as well for the whole tenor, the sterile exasperations and recalcitrances, of his treadmill life. And in fitful incursions from a world beyond his self-absorbed rancor and fearfulness—newsboys' calls in the street, a taxi driver's monologue, a reporter's cynical explanation—we discover that two hundred miles away on this same night the anarchists Sacco and Vanzetti are going to the electric chair, with protesters as far off as Paris and the Argentine making trouble about it and staging demonstrations. Payday at last, then, not only for "those two wops," so an anonymous figure in a predawn lunchroom declares: "What do I care what's right? . . . There'll be many more dead before they find out what's right."

Jim Cowan is Nathan Asch's version of a figure familiar enough in early twentieth-century writing, in both plays and novels. A recognizable descendant of the street kid Jimmy Johnson, who, in Stephen Crane's *Maggie* (1893), alternates between braggadocio swagger and a craven submission to others' judgments, he is not so brutish as Eugene O'Neill's "hairy ape" stoker (1920), nor as constitutionally tight-wound and primed to explode as the figure of Lee Harvey Oswald, riding at the head of a lurching subway train at the beginning of Don DeLillo's *Libra* (1988). In his frantic pleasure pilgrimage through New York's nighttime tawdriness, and in his virtual anonymity, Jim Cowan is like the protagonist of one of the Belgian artist Frans Masereel's modernist cartoon-novellas, the more so for Asch's spare but telling notation of the physical environments framing his character's night journey.

Except for a moment late in the second chapter when Jim stops at his family's apartment, the events of the narrative, actual or imagined, all take place in anonymous public settings: the subway, the elevated, the sidewalks and numbered streets, lunchrooms, taxi cabs, a movie palace, a dance hall, nightclubs and speakeasies. All of these have one feature in common: they are spaces of social promiscuity where troubling personal questions are not likely to be pressed, and people can mingle in a common simulation of self-importance and freewheeling adventure. But for Jim Cowan a deep panic of placelessness and desolation is never far off. Circumstances are continually closing in on him, yearned-for possibilities shut down, petty fantasies of power and triumph give way abruptly to a certainty of rejection and failure and then to counter-fantasies of violent reprisal. A soda jerk is slow to serve him. A panhandler pockets his dime and turns away without showing gratitude. Someone physically bigger shoves him aside at a street corner, and because he is afraid to strike back, humiliation veers around into hatred, and he pictures to himself satisfying responses that he doesn't dare to carry out:

> . . . he wanted to run after him, to jump on him, throw him on the ground, and kick him. He didn't know what he wanted, but with each step the guy was taking farther away from him, something more awful was happening. Somehow nothing could go on until the guy was down. Everything Jim had, everything he thought he was, was gone with the guy who had now disappeared beyond Forty-Fourth Street.

The ravaging pathology of powerlessness, in a space of life overflowing with forbidden gratifications and unattainable rewards, could not be more trenchantly evoked. Like *The Great Gatsby*'s Nick Carraway, Jim looks inside taxis and private limousines where prosperous couples lean together or hurry off to undisclosed satisfactions, and can only feel surer than ever that his waitress friend will not show up after all, that nobody will ever lean toward him or want to be with him, that there is "something wrong" with everything about him. His clothes are wrong; his manner, his appearance, his prospects, the situations and pleasures he has gone in search of—all are hopelessly wrong:

> There was something wrong in the air, in the [elevated] car, inside of him. He was born wrong, he lived wrong, he was wrong. . . . He was no one, nothing, he wasn't worth a God damn. . . . There was nowhere he really belonged. . . . No one looked at him, no one saw him, nobody in the whole world knew he was alive.

When once, he remembers, an ingenuous dance-hall pickup did take him home with her and responded with sweet eagerness to his fumbling advances, he had been miserably, shamefully impotent; "without saying a word," he had simply gone away. And when, thoroughly drunk, he for once talks back to a loud-mouthed bar character, he gets a sock in the jaw that knocks him (more or less literally) into next week.

Through the whole of *Pay Day* nearly every detail confirms the commonplaceness of all this. Jim Cowan is no freak of private disaffection but a representative citizen of a society sodden with disappointments and with shabby—or murderous—substitutions. His story is anybody's story. The waitress Helen, soon after they meet for their date and almost at once are gibing at each other in suspicion and resentment, has an extended monologue about her own multiplying difficulties with frauds, crooks, lecherous cheapskates, and mashers. Later on, out dancing, she will attach herself to another nighttime floater as casually as she started off with Jim: "Good riddance, too," he thinks, eyes and hands now grabbing after another more pliant and responsive girl named Anna. A state senator who turns up at a midtown speakeasy has only his presumed influence to distinguish him from the crowd around him; when there is a challenge to his patriotic cant about Sacco and Vanzetti—"they were Reds, weren't they? . . . There's no room for them in this country"—and a brawl threatens, he backs off as cravenly as anybody.

A voluble taxi driver hauling the party away after Jim has been knocked cold runs through the whole range of self-canceling resentments the book's characters express and enact. So tired and ·driven is he by the life he leads, harassed by family obligations and forced to work at night for weeks at a time, he tells his passengers he would as soon be dead: "I get so tired driving, keeping the damned foot on the damned accelerator, sometimes, when I get near a good strong Elevated pole I just want to shove it on, and go to hell." Or, alternatively, to kill somebody. Fed up with smart-aleck street kids who block his passage and force him to slow down, "some day," he continues, "I'm going to step on it, and smash one of them." But in the next breath he is speaking up in forlorn sympathy for "the two guys up in Boston that got burnt tonight," for their gentleness, their fight to stay alive, the chance that they are really innocent. He has even thought, with a certain relief, of going up to Boston and offering to take their place: "I've got nothing to live for, anyway." "If the public wants somebody killed," he would tell them, "well then go ahead and kill me." (But a moment later, stopped for speeding and erratic driving, he dodges a police citation by rousing the senator, drunk in the backseat, to intervene and pull rank.)

Are there, in Asch's composite vision, any alternatives to this squalid world of paydays, payoffs, payments fraudulently deferred? In the most inventive chapter in the book, "The Movie," one kind of alternative is put before us when, after a set of vaudeville acts, the theater darkens again and Jim and his waitress, still irritably taunting each other, settle back to watch the main feature. Here Asch turns abruptly away from the realistic narrative we have followed so far and unfolds a long, multisectioned prose poem evoking not the action of the film itself but the progress of a single day across the vast continental landscape, from its Atlantic coast predawn to the moonlit streets and farms, the Pullman sleepers, the city revels and deserted interior towns, the ranchlands and looming mountains, of another night's slow conclusion. It is nothing less than an ideal projection of the whole national life, freed for once from its discontents and frustrations. Every great or small transaction now goes forward in its proper place. The grand system of mills and factories, farm production and transport, dam building and road mending, Stock Exchange excitements and a church choir's midday rehearsal, functions as it was meant to, and the huge and varied population jostles publicly together or goes about its most intimate affairs in rough harmony and light-flooded peace. These twenty pageantlike pages have none of Whitman's rhythmic poetry of evocation (nor, fortunately, of Carl Sandburg's breathy lyricism). They are matter-of-fact, set down in a style closer to honest telegraphese, at times rather too suggestive of Norman Rockwell's collages of the gently typical but more often recalling the photographic bareness of a Charles Sheeler factory pastoral, the organized clutter of a street scene by John Sloan or Reginald Marsh. All this, the "movie" tells us, is what life in America could be and should be; why then doesn't it become so?

And indirectly, through two surrogate voices, another kind of alternative is indicated; it is the way of any writer honest enough to present the ordinary truth about life without falsification and distracting palliatives. An argument starts up about a current movie that has no proper story or plot, only (someone complains) "a lot of machinery, a lot of scenery, a lot of kids and that's all." Someone else argues back, in contempt: "You got to have a story, don't you? . . . You can't look when somebody's trying to be honest and show you the country you're living in, how it looks, and what's in it." Later still, on the subway, another voice is overheard talking about what has happened that night in Boston. If you tell people, this man points out, that an injustice, a crime, a horror has been committed, they will listen for a while—"because they listen to everything." But "then they would hear the name Sacco, the name Vanzetti, and they would turn away." "Oh, yes, we know about that," they would say. "We read about it in the newspapers. Some tried to get them off, some said they were guilty. Who cares?"

> Try to think of a way to reach them [the nameless subway speaker continues], these rulers of the country for whose benefit all this was arranged, as a warning, as a lesson. Somehow try to wake them up. Words mean nothing to them. They're old, stale, they have been used too much. . . . The newspapers have been screaming headlines at them for months. They read them and look elsewhere. . . . Two men are hounded and framed into death. More headlines. Always the same. The sports page is more interesting, the comic page more amusing. Why read what's under the headlines? . . .
>
> Find a way to wake them, to make them realize words. Try to talk to them, to make them understand. Do something.

What then was *Pay Day* but Nathan Asch's attempt as a novelist, at the midpoint between two terrible wars and at the onset of the country's blind plunge into the Depression, to "do something"; to give readers an honest account of the society they were really living in, "how it looks and what's in it"; to "realize" some part, at least, of the meaning of the headlined words they were numbingly awash in.

These are not alternatives the protagonist of *Pay Day* is himself capable of. For Jim Cowan, Asch reserves a single late moment of exact self-knowledge; it is a moment, however, that points only toward death and obliteration, or perhaps—an ironic parenthesis adds—"to the lunatic asylum." On his way home, stumbling toward a subway platform, for this once at least "he absolutely knew he was alive, couldn't forget it one minute, would never be able to forget it. Whatever he did he would always realize that now he was and that some day he would not be." His actual point of rest will be nothing more than the humdrum apartment where he lives with his hovering Ma and bitchy sister and where, early in the novel, sprawled out in the amniotic warmth of a soapy bathtub, he has literally regressed into infantilism:

> He stretched out, sighed very deeply, and closed his eyes. Never would he get out of the tub. To hell with dressing, to hell with dinner, and to hell with the girl he was meeting later. To stay in the tub with the warm soft water around him, breathing easily. His cheek touched his shoulder, and it felt soft like a baby's shoulder, and then without knowing what he was doing, he kissed his shoulder.

The title of this closing chapter, "Home Again," carries its own ironies. On the last page Jim is standing below the apartment, looking up at a lighted window where "poor Ma" waits up for him; but he has reached this point by way, first, of a hallucinated scene (modeled on the phantasmagoric Nighttown section of *Ulysses*) in which Ma and a peremptory judge are holding him to account in a combination courtroom and nightclub—Ma and the judge are soon dancing together, "very close"—and then of an encounter with a homeless and scared ten-year-old boy whose sleeping place for the night is a rattling subway car. Virtually the last words given to Jim in the novel are a plea for help, but spoken in the third person as if in behalf of some lost, irretrievably other, self: "Anna help him. Somebody help him." But sweet, pliant Anna is no longer there, as phantomlike in her disappearance as in her earlier surrender to him. That nameless, faceless "somebody" we understand as the unanswering icon of a profoundly negative, or empty, faith.

Jim Cowan is not Nathan Asch. But what else does this final cry give voice to but the fatalism that dogged Asch's life as a writer and gives to the failure of his career an appearance of being in some substantial measure self-inflicted? Yet it was a fatalism that in its very impersonality served to keep him alive and writing through another thirty-odd years of dwindling fortune and vanishing hope. It may be, then, that *Pay Day* finds its deepest conviction and force in Asch's hidden awareness that the sad story of Jim

Cowan's journey to the end of night might prove to be, one way or another, his own story as well.

A Note on the Sacco-Vanzetti Case

Nicola Sacco and Bartolomeo Vanzetti, on the basis of entirely circumstantial evidence, were tried and condemned to death in 1921 for the robbery and shooting of a shoe company paymaster in South Braintree, Massachusetts. What share they may have had in the actual crime has never been conclusively determined. What is certain is that there were serious irregularities in the proceedings that condemned them. Their case dragged on in the courts for several years, amid rising protestations and worldwide concern; it came to be seen as a test of basic American principles, in particular the principle of equal justice before the law. When, in the summer of 1927, a three-man panel appointed by Governor Alvan Fuller—it included the presidents of Harvard University and the Massachusetts Institute of Technology—refused to recommend returning the case to the courts, popular outrage intensified. In the weeks preceding the two men's execution, which occurred on August 22, 1927, concerned citizens of many kinds—civil libertarians, writers and intellectuals, Communists aiming to convert the cause to their own uses—converged on Boston in the hundreds, then in the thousands. A Defense Committee was formed and held outdoor rallies. There was a rash of inner-city bombings, thought to be related to the case, in New York, Philadelphia, Baltimore; the entire Boston police force was put on twenty-four-hour duty, and in Washington contingency plans were drawn up to mobilize army and marine troops.

In its final days the affair attracted the whole world's attention. Ten thousand people demonstrated on the side of the condemned men in Trafalgar Square; similar crowds marched in Paris and in Switzerland, Germany, and Argentina; in Johannesburg an American flag was burned on the steps of the Town Hall. The case drew a series of eight-column headlines in the *New York Times*. Harold Laski, the English radical, wrote to Justice Oliver Wendell Holmes, Jr., of "the immense damage" the whole affair was doing in Britain and Europe to the good name of the United States. And in Boston, joining the deathwatch outside Charlestown State Prison on the night of the execution were such prominent writers as John Dos Passos,

Malcolm Cowley, the journalist Heywood Broun, and Dorothy Parker of *The New Yorker*.

On the fiftieth anniversary of the execution, the Democratic governor of Massachusetts, Michael S. Dukakis, proclaimed Tuesday, August 23, 1977, "NICOLA SACCO AND BARTOLOMEO VANZETTI MEMORIAL DAY," and declared that in view of the prejudicial atmosphere at the time of the trial, the evident unfairness in the conduct of officials involved in the case, and the shortcomings of the appellate review system then prevailing, "any stigma and disgrace should be forever removed from the names of Nicola Sacco and Bartolomeo Vanzetti." The governor called upon "all the people of Massachusetts to pause in their daily endeavors to reflect upon these tragic events, and draw from their historic lessons the resolve to prevent the forces of intolerance, fear, and hatred from ever again uniting to overcome the rationality, wisdom, and fairness to which our legal system aspires."

Pay Day's Critical Reception

After its February 1930 publication, reviews of *Pay Day* were slow to appear; the book was not considered a major publishing event. In a short "Books in Brief" notice, *The Nation* (March 12, 1930), politically sympathetic, commented that though it was "a studied report rather than a novel," it was nevertheless "a swiftly moving, accurate, and engrossing report." "There are thousands of pimply-faced Jims in every big city," the anonymous reviewer remarked; "Mr. Asch has done an excellent study of the type." More conservative journals were less generous. The *Saturday Review of Literature*, which had given *The Office* good marks five years earlier, evidently decided not to mention *Pay Day* at all. Louis Kronenberger, in *The Bookman* (April–May 1930), gave a harsher turn to the point about Jim Cowan's typicality, commenting that it was "only the type in him which rings true; Jim's more personal thoughts and actions miss fire, and do not bring him to life." Kronenberger did praise Asch's descriptive powers, in particular his "sense of atmosphere and manners—in his downtown New York at night [and] in his speakeasy scenes."

At this point a different kind of public response overtook Asch's novel. The *New York Times* for April 18, 1930, carried a report that John S. Sumner of the Society for the Suppression of Vice, acting with a warrant from the Yorkville (Manhattan) police court, had seized twenty copies of

Pay Day from the East 53rd Street offices of Brewer and Warren and fifty more at the firm's East 24th Street warehouse and was preparing to prosecute the book on charges of obscenity. The initial complaint, according to the *Times*, had come from a children's welfare agency in Brooklyn, after a local mother's angry discovery that her child (age not given) was reading it. The Society for the Suppression of Vice was the same watchdog organization that ten years before had stopped serial publication of *Ulysses* in *The Little Review*. The attorney who came forward to defend Brewer and Warren was the noted civil liberties lawyer Morris L. Ernst, who in 1933 would successfully defend the book version of *Ulysses*, in a U.S. District Court, from charges of obscenity and from liability to seizure and confiscation.

After first forcing the Society to put in evidence a clean copy of *Pay Day*—one not already marked up to call attention to objectionable passages—Morris Ernst won a ruling on May 15, 1930, that the book was not obscene. In his verdict Magistrate Harry Goodman decreed that, considering the book as a whole, Jim Cowan's sexual behavior "is not glorified or sanctioned . . . on the contrary he is made to suffer because of his transgressions." Further, even "the immature, young, inexperienced and uninformed" might positively "benefit" from reading such a book. But in the *Times* Sunday book section four days earlier (May 11, 1930), critical reservations had already congealed into sniffy, across-the-board disapproval, the reviewer (again anonymous) declaring that "Mr. Asch has fished out the feelings of a pretty uninteresting character" and has produced "a lengthy and tedious study in mediocrity." But the *Times* critic was not willing to leave the matter at that; possibly with the court case in mind, he was irresistibly drawn to deliver his own expert judgment on the point of Asch's forthrightness about sexual feelings: "The author has taken some pains to be what is known as frank in describing Jim's abortive love affairs, [which involve] the less cerebral and spiritual aspects of love-making."

After Magistrate Goodman's decision, the Society was characterized by the *Times* as uncertain of what its next move should be. At some point, however, during the weeks following—though the *Times* seems to have lost interest and carried no further articles on the affair—*Pay Day* apparently came under at least the threat of a grand-jury citation. This, at any rate, was the assumption behind the review carried by *The New Republic* in its July 16, 1930, issue. The reviewer ("J. M.") took no pleasure in the story itself: "no illumination, no enjoyment results from reading it." But his view of its social significance was only sharpened by its troubles with self-appointed censors: "Because *Pay Day* really rebukes the metropolis as a begrimer of helplessly whirling lives, its grand-jury indictment should be applauded everywhere. A sincere sociological novel thus becomes assured of untold readers." That happy consequence never materialized. Whatever new readership the book's season of notoriety might have attracted would have had trouble finding it to buy, for neither the author nor his publisher seems to have made any further effort to keep it in circulation. In the long run it was as if Nathan Asch had anticipated some such calamity all along. In later years all he would say of the fate of his best novel was that it had been "suppressed."

10

"Everything Is All Right and Difficult"

The Poems of Frank O'Hara

A generation past the time of its creation, the "original, hydrogenic, anthropomorphic, fiscal, post-anti-esthetic, bland, unpicturesque, WilliamCarlosWilliamsian . . . definitely not nineteenth century . . . not even Partisan Review" poetry of Frank O'Hara (the self-characterization is in "Poem Read at Joan Mitchell's") is turning out to have been as classic, in the commendatory sense, as any in our still-vital Romantic tradition. As continuously as a Shelley's or a Yeats's, it reflects a rich awareness of the odds modern life keeps piling up against any "perfecting of its own nature in each thing" (the prime definition of creaturely virtue), or in each man or woman, or in mankind collectively. It does so in poetic arguments distinctive to its particular locale and epoch: New York ("most extravagant of cities" to Henry James) in the super-politicized but otherwise liberated and unbuttoned later twentieth century. So this poetry now and then explicitly reproduces the way in which, masking our most unreal terror, we have casually mouthed the names of those who in our time would assume command of modern megadeath, as if it were all a new species of media entertainment. For O'Hara politics was mostly a tiresome interruption, but he knew what he was doing (on September 17, 1959) in making "Khrushchev" the opening word of one of his most ebullient New York lyrics:

> Khrushchev is coming on the right day!
>   the cool graced light
> is pushed off the enormous glass piers by hard wind
> and everything is tossing, hurrying on up
>   this country
> has everything but *politesse*, a Puerto Rican cab driver
> says. . . .

Once touched off in this poem, legitimate anxiety about the recklessness of responsible statesmen hangs on through the brilliant city-morning scene and gives a sharper edge to the brisk repertory of Romantic attitudes: children and the beautiful young are the innocent ones, art is the thing to get excited about, the world is more various than we commonly remember, love and friendship count most, nostalgia is comforting, selfhood always flirts dangerously with darkness but can steady itself by remembering its kinship with other men of the crowd—

>   . . . Ionesco is greater
> than Beckett, Vincent said, that's what I think, blueberry
>   blintzes
> and Khrushchev was probably being carped at
>   in Washington, no *politesse*
> Vincent tells me about his mother's trip to Sweden
>   Hans tells us
> about his father's life in Sweden, it sounds like Grace
>   Hartigan's
> painting *Sweden*
>   so I go home to bed and names drift through my head
> Purgatorio Machado, Gerhard Schwartz and Gaspar
>   Gonzales, all
>   unknown figures of the early morning as I go to work

The September wind *is* "hard," hard as the life and probable fortune of the great modern city whose buildings it transforms into

> . . . ozone stalagmites
>   deposits of light

—but it is still the correspondent wind of Romantic, and Shelleyan, prophecy, and a benediction to those who can lift themselves to meet it:

> New York seems blinding and my tie is blowing up the street
> I wish it would blow off
>   though it is cold and somewhat warms my neck
> as the train bears Khrushchev on to Pennsylvania Station
>   and the light seems eternal
>   and joy seems inexorable
>   I am foolish enough always to find it in wind.

O'Hara's writing is knotted tightly enough into its time and place—Manhattan in the 1950s and early 1960s, when the city's popular institutions still worked and its special pleasures were commonly affordable—to need now as much scholarly annotation as Yeats's or Pound's. What is also true is that all its leading properties may be defined in terms of Romantic and late-Romantic (imagist, Surrealist, neo-Dada) precedent. It composes a very American and mid-twentieth-century Psalm of Life, though without Long-fellow's earnestness and verbal uniformity; a poetry of celebration and personal attachment, even if largely in the vein of parody and self-mockery. To be where "at least something's going on" is not quite all of Frank O'Hara's aim in life (or in poetry), but aim enough when the result is also a willingness to "stand[ ] erect in the spirit's glare and wait[ ] for the joining of an opposite force's breath" ("In Favor of One's Time"); a willingness—not unlike the Self's in Yeats's great "Dialogue" but deliberately under-stated—"calmly to face almost everything" ("Joe's Jacket").

[O'Hara's verse would profit from annotation even among those readers whose commentaries have helped establish "The Day Lady Died," his elegy for the singer Billie Holiday, as very nearly the surest American anthology selection of the past thirty years, yet who seem to have missed the clear logic linking all the random-seeming details of the poem's first four stanzas. Even Alan Feldman's discerning study (*Frank O'Hara*, 1979) speaks of this poem as written in opposition to "the elegiac tradition" and as being "full of irritating inconsequentialities." It is of course traditional through and through, a staged lament for an exemplary fellow artist which surrenders (as Milton in "Lycidas," Shelley in "Adonais") the poet's own imaginative identity to the ritual of grieving. And what is "inconsequential" about these details—that he knows the exact departure and arrival times of the train taking him to dinner that night but does not know "the people who will feed me"; that only once has he ever heard his bank teller's given name and only once *not* been made to wait for his own identity and balance to be double-checked; that he accepts the task of finding out about "the poets / in Ghana" however drably printed up—in speaking to a life (Billie Holiday's) spent in solitude of spirit and ultimately in self-rejection, and a death that reaches its grievers only in the headlines of a newsstand tabloid? Aren't isolation and anonymity the consistent burden here? Doesn't, also, the serious work of choosing appropriate gifts for valued friends—Verlaine illustrated by Bonnard (!) or Lattimore's elegant Hesiod and three controversial off-Broadway plays; imported Italian liqueur and imported cigarettes—qualify and prepare him to be the right celebrant of Lady Day's heartstopping gift as a blues interpreter?]

Claims for Frank O'Hara's weight and scope should be entered as discreetly as for others in his poetically favored but privately watchful and circumspect American generation (Merrill, Merwin, Ashbery, Ammons, for starters). He does not—like Shelley, like Yeats—seek out heroic trials, or crave some posting of the odds beyond his own time's radical uncertainty and demoralization. He is unapologetic about wanting to live as long as possible inside a dream of life in which "all pain is extra" ("Ode (to Joseph Lesueur on the Arrow That Flieth By Day)"); a life resolutely devoted to love, art, festival, courtesy, though never to mere comfort or correct taste. His effort is to appear to be writing from the very quick of continuous, unsegmented life, his own and the outreaching world's. "I don't have to make elaborately sounded structures," he announces in the first paragraph of "Personism: A Manifesto" (September 3, 1959); "I don't even like rhythm, assonance, all that stuff. You just go on your nerve"—a principle confirmed in the variousness of his self-dramatizations, in which reversals and self-evasions continually augment the illusion of human presence.

His vision seems sharpest a little off the center of things. "A step away" is best, distancing what matters most so as to get a truer purchase on it.[1]

---

1. "For every description is an externalization of the object: a step aside so as to see it": Joseph Brodsky, *Less Than One: Selected Essays* (1986), 340.

During the treacherous "confessional" interval in contemporary American poetry, Keats's negative capability became more needful than ever, and O'Hara—who alludes to it directly in "Personism"—effectively reinvented it as a working method. "How I hate subject matter," he writes in a more contentious mood ("To Hell With It"), and there is now and then an overindulgence in the clichés of post-Eliot, post–*Partisan Review* anti-intellectualism. Deciding, with fellow New Yorkers, that "we don't like Lionel Trilling" or even "Henry James so much" is good fun, especially when followed by "we like Herman Melville" and then, "we just want to be rich / and walk on girders in our silver hats" ("Personal Poem"). But being against "ideas" simply because "ideas are obscure and nothing should be obscure tonight" intrudes something impertinent into a ceremony that does not need it ("Poem Read at Joan Mitchell's," celebrating a marriage—wouldn't any marriage be a little better off for a few shared ideas?), and the subordinate clause's turn of phrase in describing the consequences of a too-intense absorption in art at the expense of life ("it seems they were all cheated of some marvelous experience / which is not going to be wasted on me": "Having a Coke With You") has, even in context, an overtone of aggressive self-approval. Such attitudes, we know, are in the grand American tradition of come-off-it populism, but as much as others they need to be captured afresh, as they are in the detail of "A Young Poet" about "feel[ing] the noise of art abate, in the silence of life," or in the direct Whitmanism of "Poem: 'À la recherche de Gertrude Stein' " (cf. Whitman's "Of the Terrible Doubt of Appearances"):

> sick logic and feeble reasoning are cured
> by the perfect symmetry of your arms and legs

Disclaimers notwithstanding, O'Hara does write on subjects. Mostly they are conventionalized subjects matching the conventionalized occasions that draw him out. He writes small, direct love poems that on the whole (to borrow what Artemus Ward said of George Washington) don't slop over, even when sentimental.[2] He writes poems for and about artists, invariably

---

2. For O'Hara's own vision of the Matter of America—"the beautiful history"—and of the godfather of its republican self-renewal, there is the neatly argued "On Seeing Larry Rivers' 'Washington Crossing the Delaware' at the Museum of Modern Art": ("See how free we are! as a nation of persons."). The six-page discussion of this poem in James E. B. Breslin, *From Modern to Contemporary* (1984), and indeed the O'Hara chapter as a whole, suggest as well as anyone has to date the complexity and suppleness of O'Hara's lyric style.

expressing his gratitude. Painters—Jane Freilicher, Grace Hartigan, Red Grooms, Larry Rivers, Pollock, De Kooning—are regularly greeted as collaborators and kindred spirits; it is granted that musicians are sometimes frightening because what they can do can seem, in some moods, "to punish [us]"; but miracle-working dancers, including the one he is in love with, are only to be praised ("Ode to Tanaquil Leclerc," the Vincent Warren poems). Also there are marriage poems and party poems—occasions of refashioned community and the breaking of bread, or bottles, with friends; poems honoring dead precursors ("Second Avenue: In Memory of Vladimir Mayakovsky"), dead movie stars ("For James Dean"), dead friends ("The 'Unfinished': In Memory of Bunny Lang"); poems for friends who may need cheering up ("Fantasy: dedicated to the health of Allen Ginsberg"); poems about Emily Dickinson's great subject of the seasons and their ruthless, life-nurturing changes ("Aus Einem April," "(July Is Over And There's Very Little Trace)"). There are Romantic voyage poems, such as an American Shelley would write:

> a fleece of pure intention sailing like
> a pinto in a barque of slaves
> who soon will turn upon their captors
> lower anchor, found a city riding there
> of poverty and sweetness paralleled
> among the races without time,
> and one alone will speak of being
> born in pain
> and he will be the wings of an extraordinary liberty.
> ("Ode to Michael Goldberg")

And everywhere there are poems, and passages in poems, about the virtue of attaching oneself to the astonishing energy and variety of New York City by day or night, "the feeling of life and incident pouring over the sleeping city" ("Joe's Jacket"). O'Hara has, on the surface, the look of a poet with eyes and feelings only for what is directly to hand and of merely personal moment; but he is in fact that rarity among his contemporaries, a writer able to suggest—with what our most precisely tactful writer of criticism, John Updike, pinpoints as the "openness, dailiness, intimacy, and odd control of it all"—the very substantial attraction and pleasure of modern big-city life, its inexhaustible power as a human environment to reanimate and reawaken.

We see soon enough that "just going on nerve" is a controlled pose like any other. O'Hara's sense of design in poetry, of how to frame and when to break off, follows on a studious apprenticeship to French modernism in particular—Apollinaire, Eluard, Reverdy are major presences—and to the new masters of painting and sculpture he knew and worked with through the 1950s and early 1960s. (In the decade after 1955 O'Hara organized and wrote catalogues for contemporary exhibitions at the Museum of Modern Art: Pollock, Motherwell, David Smith, among others.) Yet he gives up a good deal in pursuing the phantom of immediacy. He gives up not only the counter-satisfactions of a sustained metrical eloquence—his longest poems, like "Second Avenue" and "Biotherm," seem to me his unsteadiest in execution—but also, most of the time, the power that can come with the elaboration of a single extended figure; the exception is, again, the cumulative figure of the city itself. And he is not consistently in command of his shape-changer's art. Even in shorter lyrics that "odd control" is not always maintained. Sometimes, with confidence in your eventual rewards, you follow along through poems that sprawl and sideslip and never do properly recover, to find at last that it was almost (but not quite) for the sake of a single line, as in the mock epithalamion read at Joan Mitchell's: "and there is no noise like the rare silence when you both sleep. . . ."

There is also, with O'Hara, an antithetical muse to be reckoned with, a smotherer of everything wind-lifted and liberating, whose spectral presence looms up in several poems and with whom, I think, he never did have it out to any conclusion. This is the mother-figure who "flew in from Des Moines / with her dog" and ruined "the whole damn vacation" ("Summer Breezes"). Even in the beguiling "Ave Maria"—"Mothers of America / let your kids go to the movies! / get them out of the house so they won't know what you're up to"—she is pictured taking her final revenge when, the nonreturning prodigal son's advice having fallen on deaf ears,

> . . . the family breaks up
> and your children grow old and blind in front of a TV set
>
> seeing
> movies you wouldn't let them see when they were young

"All things are tragic / when a mother watches!" goes one strange, awkward dream poem ("There I could never be a boy") in which the poet takes to himself the armored "speed and strength" of a powerful horse—"a frightened black mare," no less—"and she never threw me." There is, in short, a radically abridged family romance playing itself out through a considerable portion of O'Hara's writing. No doubt it too, as well as the collective apprehensiveness of the age, explains why his mask of self-limitation sometimes seems an anguished natural grimace.

But he is consistently a poet and gets his own back, family-romance-wise, in a brilliant condensation of Blake's "Mental Traveler" myth:

> I hardly ever think of June 27, 1926
> when I came moaning into my mother's world
> and tried to make it mine immediately
> by screaming, sucking, urinating
> and carrying on generally
> it was quite a day
> I wasn't proud of my penis yet, how did I know how to act? . . .
> ("Ode to Michael Goldberg")

There is a rough wisdom, finally, in Frank O'Hara's lyric address to all that gathers in the recesses of our ordinary lives, and of all we do, all the shifts we are put to, both to embrace this hidden life and to keep from drowning in it. A rueful wisdom about love, for example, as even in the ripest swell of it he can stand off—off from himself, too—without suspending delight:

> and each reason for love always
> a certain hostility, mistaken
> for wisdom
>   exceptional excitement
> which is finally simple blindness
> (but not to be sneezed at!) like
> a successful American satellite
> ("Ode to Michael Goldberg")

One other section of the same poem—a poem greeting new life by reviewing, synoptically, the testing places of his own already half-expended one— expresses with unusual force (despite one risky *boutade*) the sensibility and, among his contemporaries, uncommon personal honesty that in combination seem to me to have served poetry itself about as well as one may hope for nowadays:

A couple of specifically anguished days
make me now distrust sorrow, simple sorrow
especially, like sorrow over death

it makes you wonder who you are to be sorrowful
over death, death belonging to another
and suddenly inhabited by you without permission

you moved in impulsively and took it up
declaring your Squatters' Rights in howls
or screaming with rage, like a parvenu in a Chinese laundry

disbelieving your own feelings is the worst
and you suspect that you are jealous of this death

If it is indeed, as Yeats said, by way of an argument with our antithetical selves that poetry comes forth, an argument in which the responsive life in us discovers and confronts its most dogged adversaries, Frank O'Hara, too, belongs with the poets. As much as charm or good humor, celebration without self-deception is his lyric art's determining ethos. Coming to expression through attitudes of grateful acceptance in the least forgiving of great modern cities, it seems to me a main reason for that art's uncommon trustworthiness.

11

Life "Upstate"

Edmund Wilson's American Memoir

A year before his death in 1972, the American critic and man of letters Edmund Wilson published a book dealing with the isolated district in northern New York State, on the western edge of the Adirondack wilderness, where sixty-some years earlier he had regularly spent summer holidays and to which, around 1950, he began returning each year for the summer season. It was not the first time he had written about this district, more particularly about the house itself, spacious and solidly built, to which he had come as a boy with his family and an active crowd of cousins, aunts, and great-aunts reassembled from several different American cities and states. In an essay of 1933 entitled "The Old Stone House," written during the grinding national crisis of the Depression, he looked back admiringly to "the amplitude and completeness of the place," which dated from the earliest years of American independence; according to family records, one of the first notable occurrences in it was a memorial service following the death of General Washington in 1799. Built in the opening stages of the young republic's vast westward expansion, this house represented (Wilson wrote) something more than a practical solution to the problem of shelter in a frontier settlement. Four or five years in the making, with stone walls a foot and a half thick, hand-forged nails securing massive beams and rafters, a columned front porch and full-length upper balcony, it symbolized nothing less than "an attempt to found a civilization." As late as the years around 1900, when Wilson himself first knew it, it had not altogether lost this original character. It remained the home of "a big old-fashioned family that had to be"—while in residence—"a city in itself." As Wilson recalled, "not merely did it house a clan; the whole life of the community passed through it."

But by 1932 that local community was sharply in decline, its supporting economy severely reduced from the peak years of its early hope and promise. And the house of his childhood recollections, when Wilson traveled back that year for a short visit, seemed correspondingly diminished. Originally it had been, he remembered, "the center of the town," but now the town itself—Talcottville, in Lewis County, New York—was not much more than a few outlying farms and a scattering of houses along the state highway; and the house, now for most of the year "nothing but an unheated shell, a storehouse of unused antiques," had lost any "intimate relation" to the region around. Nevertheless, in Edmund Wilson's imagination it remained a kind of dream world. It was still the place at the end of the road that runs west and into summer, the place of "sun and air," wildness and freedom, the great good place of a still visionary delight. At the same time he felt compelled to acknowledge that in cold, harsh fact the "civilization of northern New York—why should I idealize it?" was now and (childhood memories notwithstanding) probably always had been "too lonely, too poor, too provincial."

Such was Wilson's melancholy conclusion in his retrospective essay of 1933, a conclusion that, when it appeared in book form in *Travels in Two Democracies* (1935), symbolically reinforced a whole series of descriptions of American society in the throes of economic breakdown and flagging public morale. But economic depressions pass, once they have taken their full toll in social injury and disheartenment. Economies recover, as the American economy did on a grand scale, and the spirit and confidence of the population as well, with the activism of the New Deal era and the challenge of a world-encompassing war against Hitlerite Germany and counter-imperial Japan. Even a place like Talcottville managed a modest recovery. It not only remained on the map as a town but soon enough, in the new electronic era and with an expanded federal highway system, discovered itself more accessible from outside than in times past and thus, on the whole, less lonely and cheerless for people living there. And in 1950 Wilson himself decided to reestablish his summer life in Talcottville, in the stone house of his childhood. At the age of fifty-five (the years of his life, he felt, passing more quickly than ever), his explicit concern was to create a point of permanence and continuity in the uncertain flux of his own and contemporary American existence.

With the book he eventually compiled on the foundation of this deliberate act of, at once, self-recovery and historical repossession, he used for the title the single word "Upstate," the distinctively American locution that for two hundred years has served to identify all of the State of New York lying north of, roughly, the forty-first parallel; north, that is, of the great harbor metropolis and its nearer suburbs. The double character he gave the book is effectively summed up in its secondary title: "Records and Recollections of Northern New York." It is a chronicle both of Wilson's personal concerns and interests as author and householder and of—with special emphasis on Lewis County—the character and history of the entire region west of Albany and north of the old "water-level" route to the Great Lakes and upper Middle West. Indeed, with its actively superintending protagonist and its panoramic survey of an entire historical environment, it has the qualities of a certain kind of novel; a novel that by a fullness of social vision convinces its reader of the broad general truthfulness with which it has evoked a pattern of intimate human experience under the compulsions of time and change.[1]

Edmund Wilson's earlier fame was won mainly through his voluminous critical writing: as, first, an interpreter of the achievement of the great modernist inheritors of nineteenth-century European Symbolism (in *Axel's Castle*) and of the careers and imaginations of a number of master figures

1. In recent American writing, *Upstate* may be joined to a class of books for which, rather supposititiously, a whole new classification has been thought up and given currency: the "nonfiction novel." The books in question are most often detailed reportorial accounts of public happenings—Norman Mailer's *The Armies of the Night* and *The Executioner's Song*, Truman Capote's *In Cold Blood*, and Tom Wolfe's *The Electric Kool-Aid Acid Test* are prime examples—in which the writer himself plays an active, perhaps even central, role. Some of the best of these are straightforwardly autobiographical, like *All God's Dangers* (by "Nate Shaw") or *The Autobiography of Malcolm X*. But can it really be said that the form is a new one in American writing? What after all are Thoreau's *Walden* and *The Autobiography of Benjamin Franklin* but, in these terms, nonfiction novels?

like Flaubert, Pushkin, Dickens, Ben Jonson, Bernard Shaw, and Henry
James; as a singularly trustworthy reviewer of the brilliant new literature of
the 1920s and 1930s in the United States; subsequently, as a chronicler of
modern ideological movements such as revolutionary Marxism (in *To the
Finland Station*), Western democratic liberalism, and contemporary Zionism,
and of their consequences for the present condition of life in societies under
their domination. As he had been for his friend Scott Fitzgerald an
"intellectual conscience" from the time of their student years at Princeton,
so he became a literary-critical conscience for the American community of
letters in general; a definer of performative standards and a practical court
of appeal for the common exercise of critical understanding, whether or not
one happened to agree with every opinion briskly handed down. But he also
shared with the best of his own American generation—with Fitzgerald,
Hemingway, Faulkner, Dos Passos, Hart Crane, and Allen Tate, among
others—a strong personal desire to make his mark as a literary creator as
well. From 1920 forward, along with his uninterrupted work as essayist,
reviewer, and sociological reporter, he was also writing and publishing
poems, plays, parodies, stories, and, most notably, two full-length works of
prose fiction.

These latter books—the novel *I Thought of Daisy* (1929), with its record
of Greenwich Village personages and episodes during the 1920s, and the
1940s story collection *Memoirs of Hecate County*—have not been as widely
admired as Wilson's critical writing. Nor are they of the same order of
performative expertness as the principal novels and stories of his major
contemporaries; in each, narration and authorial reflection, exposition and
judgment, hang rather awkwardly together. But it is possible to feel in
reading them that the observing and interpreting voice we are listening to
is not different in quality, not less humanely alert and interest-creating,
than the voice we hear in Wilson's best criticism; and they have, as books,
grown rather more interesting and valuable as the local patterns of life they
record recede further and further into the past. In their own fashion—one
that is essentially documentary in scope and detail—these two novels (if
that is what they are) remain oddly memorable in the account they offer of
the actual behavior of men and women in certain recognizable modern times
and places. It is to them, perhaps, more than to any other book he has
published, that in the long span of Edmund Wilson's literary career the
book *Upstate* stands closest in spirit and imaginative effect. Quite possibly it
is the strongest work in this interesting series; a book that, even with its
out-of-the-way provincial setting, is as abundantly suggestive of the forms

and pressures of American life in the decades following World War II as any report, memoir, or tract coming to us from the more publicized battle-grounds of our continuously self-revolutionizing age.

The main sequences in *Upstate* are drawn from diary-notebooks kept between 1950 and 1970; the book thus runs the circuit of Wilson's reoccupancy of the Talcottville house. It gains from this annually renewed adventure an emotional shape and plot which are lacking in other late or posthumous volumes—*A Prelude, The Twenties, The Thirties*—that reconstruct on the same notebook basis Wilson's life and interests in earlier periods. When he established himself again, at fifty-five, in what during childhood had been a place of enchantment for him, he felt uneasy at first and not fully at home, as if crowded out by the ghosts of other times. In a place once overflowing with human energy and will, the almost tangible absences were oppressive. But the old elevation of spirit he had always felt upon returning to the open, half-wild countryside around reasserts itself, and he is soon absorbed in the daily business of restoring the house and of rediscovering the neighborhood and its everyday activities—activities stimulatingly different from those of authors, publishers, reviewers and, *a fortiori*, professors.

Year by year, as the chronicle advances, we watch him making the place more and more his own again. He is no longer reminded of the past only; he fills the house once more with his own vigorous presence, his daily regimen of literary work, and whichever friends or family group he can persuade to visit him. (His Russian-born wife soon acknowledges a sharp distaste for rural isolation and comes each year only for brief intervals, if at all.) Soon he feels that he has truly "taken possession" of the house, that he is "more comfortable and myself here probably than anywhere in the world." He begins to return earlier each spring, forms new relationships with the local population, and at length becomes simply one among many in the village and through the county who go about their particular business and, when they meet, exchange wise comments on the weather (a matter of high importance in that northern farm country), on local affairs, and on the general condition of the world at large as they hear about it over the radio and through the newspapers.

But all the while time runs forward, and the region itself undergoes new and unforeseen changes, acting out its part in the vaster changes that year by year, Wilson feels, are wrenching the world at large away from him as he himself grows away from it, or out of it, into old age. And though by the end of the book the ghosts have vanished and the legendary past has been reabsorbed into a fully lived present, the burdens of aging have forced a further change in his own situation. There are rising uncertainties not only about his increasingly unstable health—his heart gives him trouble, and he will not cut back the heavy drinking that was the passe-parole of his literary generation—but also about his accustomed ways of understanding things, of picturing and interpreting events as they happen. An elegiac note comes into the book. Wilson has done what he set out to do; he has restored the old family house and built an active life within it; but increasingly he sees himself as alone and stranded, no longer much concerned with the spreading disorders all around him in the world, conscious not of the permanence and continuity he had come upstate to find but only of "the constant flow and perishable character of everything on earth." As for "upstate" itself, though in twenty years the district has in fact changed as little as any other part of the country and has held on fairly successfully to its rural neighborliness, it too appears condemned to "the swift transience of everything in the United States." What he has written, he declares in the final section of the book, shows "the gradual but steady expiration" of the old order of local life, the life he had known in childhood but equally the life recovered during the first years of his return. His complaint is not personal; he recognizes that his reactions to new developments, particularly a new democratized mobility and an ugly machine-age sprawl of cheap pleasures and comforts across the landscape, are those of "a member of a once privileged class which is being eliminated all over the world"; but a simplicity and settledness of human existence that in its angular way had matched the physical grandeur of the land itself now seems wholly beyond recall.

This personal account, however, is only half of what Wilson gives us in *Upstate*. The mass of the book is by no means merely elegiac and mournful-sounding. It takes on instead, as Wilson renews acquaintance with the region, something of the interest of a continuously rewarding archaeological excavation, delivering up treasures that reveal a whole civilization in the dynamic perspectives of historical time and change.[2] The Talcottville house itself, and its furnishings, proves to be a sort of historical museum, and the sections of the book devoted to it form an extended catalogue of the human undertakings it has witnessed since first being occupied. In a series of early chapters we are also told about various representative episodes in the region's early history. In the first half of the nineteenth century upper New York

---

2. In this regard we may place it alongside books like *Apologies to the Iroquois*, on the Indians of New York State, and *O Canada*, about the United States's great and largely unknown neighbor to the north, which were also by-products of Wilson's act of returning upstate.

State came to be known nationally as the "burnt-over" district, by reason of the outbursts of sectarian religious fervor that regularly swept across it; and Wilson reviews in succession several of the old charismatic churches and religious communities—Shakers, Mormons, Mennonites, Hard-Shell Baptists, Footwashers, Nothingarians, Oneida Perfectionists, Lily Dale Spiritualists—that flourished in times past. He recovers the journal of a stiff-necked New England clergyman, a product of Calvinist Yale, who in 1802 described, with horror, the queer egalitarian barbarism of the original Lewis County settlements; "a mixture," this clergyman wrote, "of all the physical and moral evils that can well be conceived of," but also of a formidable independence, pride, and hope, where—amid what would seem to be spirit-destroying squalor—"every countenance indicates pleasure and satisfaction. . . . I do not know that I have seen an unhappy person for ninety miles on this river."

Wilson describes, too, and goes to inspect for himself, several ruined or restored mansions built in the early days of settlement, and comments again on the failed dream of civilization they represent; a failure that corresponds to the particular history of Talcottville, blighted almost from the start by the regular disappointment of the hopes of its founders and their heirs that it would soon become a prosperous canal, or factory, or, later, railroad center. He reviews also a good deal of family history, giving a detailed account of the life of an older woman cousin who made a career for herself in medicine, as well as of various lawyers, doctors, businessmen, and minor political officers on the male side. When we join these family biographies to the portraits of present-day Talcottville friends and neighbors with their sturdy competence and tenacity of life, and to the sketches of literary friends (Hemingway, James Thurber, Vladimir Nabokov, Van Wyck Brooks), along with summaries of new and old books he is reading and the distinctive personalities of their authors, what takes form before us is nothing less than a latter-day, democratic *Plutarch's Lives*. It is a Plutarch turned provincial in its main focus, yet not without openings to the great world and to major history. Or—among American precedents—what takes form is a contemporary *Specimen Days*: *Upstate* has much in common, in its imaginative design, with that vivid prose notebook of present diversions and recollected scenes and worthies that comes to us from Walt Whitman's later life.

Like Whitman he is always interested in other writers, other practitioners of his own line of work. One of Edmund Wilson's discoveries is of the considerable part upstate New York has played, though lacking the reputation of New England and the South, in American literary history. Wilson himself, participating in a Harold Frederic celebration in the city of Utica, recording gossip about Ezra Pound's return visit to Hamilton College at Clinton in 1969, or keeping track of literary neighbors like the Marcelin brothers from Haiti and the historical novelist Walter Edmonds, soon begins to do his part to maintain this regional tradition. The emphasis on local literary productiveness fits, in turn, into the general myth of the book— which is that "upstate" was once the domain of a free and flourishing people whose way of life survives, against adversity, in a certain robustness and self-sufficiency among not a few of their modern descendants. Those who know American "regional" writing generally, and the broader testimony of books like *The Country of the Pointed Firs* and *Winesburg, Ohio* (to say nothing of certain masterly fictions of Hawthorne and Faulkner), will recognize the kinds of imaginative idealization at work in such passages.

Yet as with these earlier American classics, the strength of *Upstate* as a record of life is in the fullness, the matter-of-fact honesty, with which the other side of the story is told. Despite extraordinary summer skies and the beauty of the long brilliant autumn, the Talcottville district is really rather bleak and inhospitable. It is surrounded by wild uplands that, Wilson thinks, "should never have been cleared at all"; marginal lands dotted now with abandoned farms, broken-down commercial buildings, and the scars of fly-by-night mining and milling ventures that went bankrupt almost before they were launched. The "civilization" Wilson has re-created in imagination was, he realizes, an affair of two or three generations at most, and it was crossed from the beginning by violence, by property quarrels and litigations, by unresolvable family feuds and antagonisms. Its grinding winters, which sometimes keep their grip on the land until into June, are hardly to be thought of—and Wilson always regrets giving in to the impulse to push the date of his return forward into early May or April. Somehow the temper of those who have survived these conditions corresponds. Even the most capable and resourceful of the upstate population seem always to have lived (so Wilson describes the Oneida community) "at an angle with the world."

And present circumstance directly continues what was true in the past. A vein of violence and degradation lying at the heart of things comes regularly to the surface in Wilson's attentive chronicle. The major events of local life each year appear to be a series of grisly accidents—automobile crashes, injuries from malfunctioning farm machinery, even murders—along with the hurts and sufferings of people trapped inside failed careers, bad marriages, and a fundamental cultural unhealthiness and demoralization. Talcottville and Lewis County provide no refuge from the peculiar ferocity of modern life. The world in which, in 1953, Wilson's infant daughter is nearly struck down along a village road by a reckless local driver and seventeen years later is badly hurt in an automobile accident in Maine; in which on every holiday weekend his village chauffeur (he himself refuses to learn to drive) lugubriously reports the latest body count in the nationwide traffic slaughter; in which news shockingly arrives of Hemingway's suicide in Idaho; in which old friends fall into violent quarrels over the senseless war in Vietnam, the countryside fills up with John Birch Society posters demanding impeachment of the humanitarian Chief Justice of the United States, a nearby strategic airbase and radar tracking station maintain a round-the-clock patrol of the Arctic frontier with Soviet Russia, and Wilson's own house and grounds fall prey day or night to the vandalism of adolescent hotrodders and motorcycle gangs with nothing else to do to pass the time—this world, as described in *Upstate*, seems one and the same wherever you enter it.

The great theme of the book is one with a long ancestry in the literature of the United States, a theme descending from the initial colonization to the latest fantasy projection of the way Americans live now, or wish to live. It is the old American dream of a better life grounded in a reawakened civility and brotherhood—as in Governor Winthrop's "city on a hill" and all its idealized successors—held up against the moral-civil anarchy and institutional tyrannization that perpetually threaten to supervene and take control. This theme is rendered in *Upstate* the more effectively because it is lodged in the common details of lives and events observed at first hand, because it is not apocalyptic in presentation but familiar and personal. An isolated episode in the closing pages provides a final instance of the book's underlying unity of witness. It is an episode that symbolically rounds out the whole documentary account of the author's twenty-year effort to give his life, as he ages, an encompassing coherence; to connect past with present, and his own long career with the history and circumstance it originally sprang from. The year is 1970. An unidentified American boy, apparently a drop-out from some college, turns up unannounced on Wilson's doorstep in Talcottville. Wilson finds it hard to discover what the boy (who, it seems, "had really read some of my books") is looking for:

> He had $3,000, he said, and was going to Austria without any idea of what he was going to do there. His family had originally been German, and he has studied and read some German. He said he was uncomfortable in the United States, and I think what he really

wanted was to get somewhere—though not Germany—where German was spoken and which would be in that respect somehow native to him.

Doesn't this episode confirm in miniature what the whole diverse chronicle has made poignantly clear; confirm it, and give it a new, matter-of-fact forlornness? The "upstates" we still dream of in America appear to lie farther and farther afield, and our secret hope of making our way back to them grows more fantastic with every passing year.[3]

3. Nevertheless, in November 1980 the American electorate chose for President a man—the oldest ever to assume the office—who made that wished-for return the main theme of his triumphant national campaign.

PART III

12

Culture and Consciousness, 1860–1915

The Onset of the Modern

In any modern society or era the intellectual life bearing directly on literary creation is, broadly speaking, twofold. There is the collateral territory where philosophers, scientists, members of the certified intellectual professions do their work—work of a kind that persistently challenges literary imaginations to vindicate in some fashion their own centrifugal existence. It is against the rivalry, if not active resistance, of this other realm of published discourse that "defenses of poetry" have seemed required of every new literary move-ment and epoch. So Nathaniel Hawthorne had felt in offering ironic apologies for being a mere writer of storybooks, and so in the generation that came of age after the Civil War did those writers of fiction—most notably William Dean Howells and Henry James—who published defenses of the initially controversial tactics of literary realism. But there is also the booming, buzzing world of popular understanding, its audible transactions less ordered and rationalized than those of trained intellect but more unintermitting in actual influence; a world that through its countervailing participation in all the languages of human exchange has its own corrosive ways of both stimulating literary ambition and holding it to moral account. In the shaken, uncertain years after the American Civil War, each of these vital streams of national consciousness, the professional and the popular, appeared to have gone rather abruptly over its banks. Each had entered a critical phase of displacement and redirection, for which the turmoil of the war itself was both portent and effective cause.

It would be Gertrude Stein's judgment sixty years later that with the Civil War America had begun creating the twentieth century. In more ways than one the convulsions of 1861–65 became, as Charles and Mary Beard were to argue in the 1920s (and as James McPherson, Gore Vidal, and Garry Wills have recently reaffirmed), a "second American Revolution," and our first evidence for continuing to think so is in the testimony of those who lived through it and beyond it. Historians looking back over the whole cycle of conflict can sort out its moments and actions of decisive significance and identify what in the aftermath proved to be the decisive new trends. The understanding voiced by contemporaries is likely to be less structured and differentiated but nonetheless grounded in actuality. Through the half decade of the Civil War there was, above all, the massive effort of concentrating material resources, productive capacity, and the practical and spiritual energies of whole populations upon the continentwide struggle; an effort that, reempowered in the victorious North by a systematic program of national consolidation and expansion (railroad building, subsidized wartime contracts, the new release of public lands signalized by the Homestead Act), committed the country to the most rapid material, industrial, technological development possible.

It was a development, a cultural as well as economic transformation, that may be traced not merely in census reports but in the imaginative experience of living people. Its principal victim was the old localized, sectarian-provincial ordering of consciousness, now inexorably shunted into margins and backwaters of social influence. Not of course without confusion and strain, not without counterviolences of resistance and repudiation (as to the legal ending of slavery) that a century later have not yet reached resolution, the epoch-defining processes subsumed in what historians have latterly called the *nationalization*, the *incorporation*, the *reinstitutionalization*, and, concurrently, the *professionalization* of American life and culture were now set on an irreversible course. Decade by decade after 1860 both reasoned understanding and popular feeling moved forward in the United States under the coercions of a steady and prodigious growth—financial panic or depression in every decade between 1870 and 1910 hardly broke the ascending curve of it—in societal wealth, numbers, integration, and power.

A handful of instances must serve to document, beginning with the war period itself, this suddenly materializing sense of change, overwhelmingly confirmed in the years that followed. Looking back half a century to the bleak winter before Vicksburg and Gettysburg, Henry Adams, in the *Education*, recalled the astonishment that from his diplomatic outpost in London he had felt at, across the Atlantic, the "first faint flush" of a new and specifically "imperial" consolidation of energy: "Little by little, at first only as a shadowy chance of what might be . . . one began to feel that somewhere behind the chaos in Washington power was taking shape; that it was massed and guided as it had not been before." The military consequences of such power became apparent soon enough as the campaigns of 1863 and 1864 unrolled. The long-run organizational and, ultimately, moral consequences forcibly caught Adams's attention on his disillusioned return, at the end of the 1860s, to the America of General Grant's administration and the Erie Railroad and Gold Conspiracy scandals. These newest patterns of Washington and New York life were a clear signal that the rules of social action had somehow changed since the time (in this historiographic myth) when men of virtue like Adams's presidential grandfather and great-grandfather could win high office and rationally oversee the country's development. The same patterns were not a bit less disturbing to Walt Whitman, whose exalted hope for an America that would exemplify "the sanest, highest freedom" he now perceived as under massive assault by formidable new antagonists: the depravity of the dominant business classes, the associated corruption of government service and the tainting even of the judiciary, the robbery and scoundrelism—"respectable as much as nonrespectable"—of everyday city life and its thickening miasma of hypocrisy, fraud, and hollowness of heart. (The harsh terms are Whitman's own, in his 1871 manifesto, *Democratic Vistas*.) To Whitman both the spiritual purgation of the war years and the precious legacy of an "all-varied, all-permitting, all-free theorem of individuality" were in danger of systematic betrayal, leaving behind only the headlong material expansion.

Much the same judgments fill out the panorama of contemporary life in which, two years later, Mark Twain and Charles Dudley Warner made the liveliest and bluntest of responses to the novelist John W. DeForest's call in 1868 for a "great American novel," a novel that would address itself comprehensively to the national condition. In nothing perhaps is their collaborative project *The Gilded Age* (1873) more remarkable than in providing a definitive name for a cultural era that had just begun to make clear its dominant character. A generation later the New York critic and social analyst John Jay Chapman was in no doubt about the historical logic of these years. If "the salient fact in the history of the last quarter-century," Chapman wrote in *Causes and Consequences* (1898), "is the growth and concentration of capital" (a process made feasible, Chapman noted, by the new railroad and telegraph networks), the underlying strategies of concentration for purely material advantage, and of corporate organization and countrywide monopoly, were arts acquired and initially mastered in the Civil War. The corruption of public life followed as a matter of course. Power itself, in every compartment of society, had simply, by virtue of the war experience, been "condensed and packaged for delivery," a phenomenon not lost on those bent on securing the advantages of power in postwar society.

2

This unprecedented condensing and packing in the essential organization of life—this long march of plutocratic centralization, as Brooks Adams celebrated it in the hard-edged historiography of *America's Economic Supremacy* (1900) and *The New Empire* (1902)—inevitably took toll of private sensibilities. A new civilization seemed to be generating a new order, or new aggravation, of human uncertainty and discontent. At the same time older attitudes fundamental to the distinctive American-democratic ethos recoiled seemingly out of control upon a population that had grown up under their bracing stimulus. What during Andrew Jackson's presidency the French observer Alexis de Tocqueville had already identified as a feverish national "restlessness" (*Democracy in America*, II, II, xiii) now fixed itself in popular consciousness as a social pathology requiring scientific treatment, as with the "American nervousness" diagnosed in 1881 by the New York neurasthenist Dr. George Beard. And what the revived Protestant introspection of the transcendentalist era had held up as a supreme ethical model and goal, the rule of "every man for himself," the new corporate capitalism sealed into place as the private discipline best suited to its own suprapersonal fulfillment. Emerson himself, though with different circumstances in mind, left behind a name for the new ethical order—an "age of severance, of dissociation," tending to all the rigors of occupational "solitude" ("Historic Notes of Life and Letters in New England")—but in a still pastoral Concord he had not imagined this ethic's ruthless promotion by the legal and moral apologists for economic expansion, or its actualization in the congested mill cities, the laissez-faire tenements and sweatshops, the debt-swamped farm communities of the new monetary-industrial leviathan.

An oppressive consciousness of displacement and separation, and of the betrayal of birthright political promises of happiness and free opportunity, lay in wait for nearly everybody not wholly in thrall to the business-coup mentality. (Mark Twain's burlesque of this mentality, in the entrepreneurial fantastications of Colonel Sellers of *The Gilded Age* and an 1892 sequel, *The American Claimant*, did not miss its underlying pathos.) Howells's point-for-point diagnosis of the national condition in *A Traveler from Altruria* (1894) merely put into plain words what his readers were coming to know as a fact of experience: that a new gulf had opened between the advantaged and disadvantaged in American life, and that more than ever fear and suspicion dominated the everyday relations of classes and interest groups. Whatever cohesion of spirit had been achieved in the crucible of the Civil War had not outlasted the victory bonfires. Beset by historical changes of this magnitude, men and women at every level of life—educated elite as well as popular masses—characteristically reach out for familiar models of consolation and recovery, or restitution; and in the America of the later nineteenth century that other grand force besides the "spirit of liberty" that Tocqueville had seen as the wellspring of American democratic behavior, the historic "spirit of religion," put its distinctive stamp on nearly every new upsurge of popular resistance, every reasoned proposal for reform and reconstruction.

Well past 1865 the old Protestant-sectarian determinations of American thought continued to shape speculative inquiry and grass-roots dissidence alike. Even the new secular philosophy of widest currency, the dour cosmic libertarianism of Herbert Spencer—whose main lesson for American disciples like the pioneering Yale sociologist William Graham Sumner was that any interference with the natural laws of social evolution, any legislated attempt to soften their impact on individual lives, threatened the welfare of the whole species—was taken up, after publication of *First Principles* in 1862, with the fervor of fresh religious conviction. In America Spencer's ponderous rationalism took on the familiar character of a popular revival movement, denouncing as immoral one after another institutional over-growth or ill-advised scheme of public intervention. (In fairness it should be observed that Sumner's own table of forbidden practices included business trusts and the new geopolitical imperialism of the Spanish-American War as well as fair-employment legislation and tax-funded charities.) Darwinism itself and the alarming principle of "the survival of the fittest," though widely interpreted as denying the authority of received religion, coalesced neatly with the inherited outlook of New World Calvinism. Religious confidence may well have been shaken if not dissolved by Darwin's science, but the vision of created life conveyed in *The Origin of Species* (1859) and *The Descent of Man* (1871) could also reinforce once-sacred certainties that only a few extraordinary souls were to be favored in life with creaturely success, and that all others somehow deserved their fate. In popular understanding the system of Darwinism came across morally, to those captivated by its mythic grandeur, as Calvinism with a scientific face—just as Social Darwinism's main ideological opponent, the altruistic socialism attractive to Howells and others (until events like the brutal stock-market collapse of 1893 and the 1894 Pullman strike forced them to choose political sides), could be shrewdly characterized by John Jay Chapman as "a religious reaction going on in an age which thinks in terms of money."

Calvinism itself, among old-stock Americans, had lost ground decade by decade to softer and easier theologies—to Deistic and Unitarian rationalism, to the revived upper-class Episcopalianism of the principal towns and cities, and to the periodic revival fervors of Methodists, Baptists, New-Light Congregationalists, and their pentecostal, perfectionist, utopian, and humanitarian offshoots. More and more after 1865 a generalized humanitarianism, a blurred faith in material progress, enlightenment, and collective benevolence, settled into place as the religion of those pretending to taste and education. (This is the popular background for a series of problem novels of the decade 1886–96—among others, Howells's *The Minister's Charge*, Edward Eggleston's *The Faith Doctor*, H. H. Boyesen's *Social Strugglers*, and Harold Frederic's *The Damnation of Theron Ware*—all dramatizing the retreat of the old faith before the constrictions, and temptations, of the new materialism.) The old Puritan moral severity, however, held fast as a weapon of last resort; new social frictions promptly brought it out of its scabbard. Julia Ward Howe's Grand Army of the Republic anthem—"He has loosed the fateful lightning of his terrible swift sword," "He is sifting out the hearts of men before his judgment seat"—spoke intimately to a population that still addressed itself to conflict in the exalted if not always clarifying language of Revelation, projecting every crisis as a return to Armageddon and every public campaign as a struggle for the nation's soul. The tenacity and persistence of this inherited frame of judgment best explain the primacy in both popular and professional thinking of millennialist and utopian responses to the institutionalized depravity, as it seemed to others besides Whitman and Mark Twain, of the new age.

During the 1880s and 1890s three books in particular, each a best-seller, tapped the enduring American instinct for, at once, prophetic outrage and evangelical hopefulness. To Henry George millennial anticipations were as natural as breathing, and they were equally so with his popular audience. Admirers of his *Progress and Poverty* (1879) were not simply persuaded by George's arguments about economic inequity. They were converted to them, and to promises of a future when neither business cycle nor survival of the entrepreneurial fittest but the Golden Rule would regulate human exchange. Conversions, however short-lived, followed also on the experience of reading Edward Bellamy's futuristic romance, *Looking Backward* (1888). There the nightmare (literally, for the protagonist) of 1880s capitalism vanishes before the heavenly city of A.D. 2000, a property-owner's paradise of technological innovation and obedience-disciplined efficiency—its wage laborers docile as domestic servants. The degree to which Henry Demarest Lloyd's exposé of the Standard Oil trust, in *Wealth Against Commonwealth* (1894), spoke to the same evangelical-utopian habit of mind is apparent in a contemporary reviewer's praise of its "noble argument on behalf of industrial Christianity." The melodrama of Lloyd's indictment, sharpened by his vigorous phrase-making—his model for style was Emerson's epigrammatic plainspokenness—was ultimately in the service of one more American vision of social redemption. Like the old Calvinism, it gave voice in particular to an odd undercurrent of yearning for an escape from solitary powerlessness through sublimation within some larger massing of historical/universal force, some reawakening of the dream of a wholly covenanted life. (Can we observe a comparable imaginative plot in Henry James's *Portrait of a Lady* and the paradoxes of his idealistic heroine's search for a significant life, or in the recondite speculations of Henry Adams, who searched boldly for a single rule or law to unriddle all history but never stopped feeling that the highest personal good would be to submit individual intelligence to some overmastering historical purpose?)

Lloyd, who at Columbia College in the 1860s had subscribed to Professor Francis Lieber's economic liberalism, was alone among these reformer-prophets in being seriously attracted to the cause and ideology of socialism, though put off by what he saw as the rank material-mindedness of its American adherents. Beyond specific proposals for political and economic reform, socialism's great appeal was its suitability to the spiritual crisis of the new corporate-industrial age. Its transcendentalizing promise was of a new mass consciousness in which, Lloyd wrote late in life, all particular reforms would be for the sake of one loftier reform, "the self-creation of a better individual [by] putting him to work as his own God at the creation of a better society." (Understanding the apprehensions of those with the money to buy his books, Lloyd also argued for socialism as the best way of regaining "social control.") With George and Bellamy, on the other hand, visions of a reformed future have on examination an odd resemblance to structures of human relationship in the fast-disappearing preindustrial past. An evident subtext in their writings is an unsubduable nostalgia for some "world we have lost." What after all supported the social equity each prophesied if not certain idealized memories of preindustrial New England village life or of the bluff freemasonry of new Western settlements before speculative profiteering took absolute command? A comparable nostalgia became a staple of the new prose fiction. In Mark Twain's Mississippi Valley writings and George Washington Cable's Creole tales, in the New England genre studies of Harriet Beecher Stowe and Sarah Orne Jewett, but equally in the American evocations of Henry James's *Washington Square* and *The Europeans*, a warmth of affection for the relative stability of earlier manners more than balances the satirizing of provincial narrowness. So, too, Howells and Edith Wharton, in late novels like *The Vacation of the Kelwyns* and *The Age of Innocence* (each published in 1920 but set in the 1870s), are essentially forgiving of rigidities of attitude they had earlier pilloried. Sooner or later, in the bewildering onslaught of contemporary history, certain stranded formations and obsolete simplicities of human coexistence reentered political and storytelling imaginations alike as possessions dangerously squandered and essential to recover.

3

A new sense of chronic social crisis; unprecedented challenges to paramount beliefs and values, most of all to the old balance of monitored selfhood and historical, or providential, or evolutionary, expectation; a secularized evangelicalism that instinctively measured events and prospects against some transcendent perfection of justice, along with new scientized ideologies that seemingly opposed spiritual aspirations with hard biological or economic fact; a pervasive nostalgia, matching a pervasive civil anxiety, for the simple egalitarianism attributed to times past—these intuitions and themes suffusing popular consciousness in the United States after 1865 were equally preoccupying for that first generation of university-based scholars who in the same years were systematically carrying out the professionalization, and full secularization, of the whole project of disciplined inquiry.

In background and early experience the men (as they almost exclusively were) of this intellectually rededicated generation were much like their more popular—and populist—contemporaries. (George, Bellamy, and Lloyd all at some point in the 1890s, like Hamlin Garland and Edgar Lee Masters among the younger writers, nourished hopes of an alliance with the Populist insurgence in national politics.) The resemblance is closest with those who established in American universities the new degree subjects of history, sociology, personality psychology, and—in inchoate form—cultural anthropology. Bellamy and Lloyd were sons of clergymen; so also were the influential Chicago sociologists William I. Thomas and, theological school training behind him, Albion Small. William Graham Sumner was ordained as an Episcopal minister before introducing Spencerism at Yale (where the maverick Thorstein Veblen heard him lecture); Sumner's chief ideological antagonist, Lester Ward (U.S. Geological Survey and Brown University) was a clergyman's grandson; the fathers of Richard T. Ely (Johns Hopkins, Wisconsin) and Simon Patten (Pennsylvania), prime movers in the founding of the American Economic Association and in the attack on laissez-faire fundamentalism, had been rigidly devout Presbyterians. The father of the labor economist John R. Commons (Wisconsin) was a Quaker abolitionist and, eventually, Christian Scientist; Commons himself, along with the Chicago social philosopher (and clergyman's son) George Herbert Mead, had attended Oberlin College in Ohio—where Thomas taught briefly in the 1890s—and Veblen, Carleton College in Minnesota, each a stronghold of midwestern Congregationalism. It may be noted that the members of this generation who became the most influential administrators within the new university system—Presidents Eliot of Harvard, White of Cornell, Gilman of Johns Hopkins, Harper of Chicago, Carey Thomas of Bryn Mawr—were, by contrast, the offspring of merchants and public officers.

It is impossible to mistake the evangelical trace across this "cognitive revolution," as it has been called, in late nineteenth-century American thought. (One product was the natural though politically undeveloped alliance between university-based social activists and the Social Gospel movement in liberal Protestantism.) Richard Ely, whose *Social Aspects of*

Christianity appeared in 1889, spoke for the majority in remembering his initial sense of mission as "a burning desire to set the world right." More specifically he defined his generation's intellectual task as one of "fulfill[ing] the Second Commandment"—but fulfilling it scientifically, through empirical investigation. The moral utopianism of his vision of reform comes over clearly enough in his statement of its leading principles: "Distribution must be so shaped . . . that all shall have assured incomes, but that no one who is personally qualified to render service shall enjoy an income without personal exertion"—this moral terrorism, to be fair, in a popular article for *Forum Magazine* in 1894. Similarly, in Ely's draft platform for the new American Economic Association, unmodified laissez-faire doctrines are identified as not merely "unsafe in politics" but "unsound in morals." (Ely's personal commitment each summer to the Chatauqua movement in regenerative popular education was much in keeping.) Given both popular and educated-genteel resistance to a social science that embraced evolution and cultural relativity as axiomatic, a certain missionary zeal and stubbornness were indispensable simply to professional survival. Sumner's position at Yale was put in peril in the 1880s by the objections of the university's philosopher-president Noah Porter to classroom use of Spencer's *Principles of Sociology*. A decade later Ely himself—target of a prolonged ideological vendetta in E. L. Godkin's liberal-purist weekly, *The Nation*—was brought to public trial, at Wisconsin, for the alleged subversiveness of his social welfare thinking; at Leland Stanford in 1900 the Hopkins-trained sociologist E. A. Ross was dismissed outright for lending scholarly support to a populist-progressive legislative agenda. One special impiety charged to the new empirical methods of social inquiry was "materialism," a term of denunciation also leveled in the mid-1880s at the narrative realism of Howells's *A Modern Instance* and *The Rise of Silas Lapham*.

But in one decisive respect the new professional and academic intelligentsia had an inestimable advantage not only over popular prejudice but over rearguard defenses of idealism and cultural gentility. This was in its increasingly informed relation to contemporary European learning. (The counterpart in prose fiction was a new critical openness to the methods and moral temper of Balzac and Flaubert, George Eliot, Zola, and Tolstoy.) America's extraordinary economic and technological expansion meant, inevitably, a continual broadening and intensifying of contacts with world culture and with movements of thought elsewhere initiated and developed. In the 1780s no one would have thought of inviting Immanuel Kant to transport his revolutionary philosophic message to the New World republic; no one in

America knew there was any such message to be received. Sixty years later the sudden American vogue of Thomas Carlyle, highly profitable to Carlyle, came about only through the accident of Emerson's enthusiastic promotional effort, and Emerson himself could never persuade Carlyle of the advantages on both sides of an American lecture tour. But by 1909, even before *The Interpretation of Dreams* was translated into English, Sigmund Freud had been invited to lecture at Clark University, the New England Johns Hopkins. As after 1900 there would not again be a major international war without American intervention (beginning with Theodore Roosevelt's peacemaking between Russia and Japan in 1905), so there would not again be an important development in European thought or expression without, promptly enough, its American adaptation—or preemptive transformation.

Among the founders of university-level inquiry in the United States after 1865, nearly everyone had studied at a German university and had returned armed with the archival realism of German historical scholarship and, not less important, a keen admiration for the new imperial-German commitment to a guided social welfare policy. The Germanic model, trained intelligence offering its professional findings to the whole civil commonwealth as well as within its own circle of learning, was a main influence in the fundamental late-century shift in sociocultural authority from a localized legal and ministerial elite to a national meritocracy of competitively trained specialists. But it was an influence that also worked to reinforce familiar expectations. The new scholarly disposition blended frictionlessly with the long-established tenor of American intellectual life as Tocqueville and others had perceived it: activist, practical, and oriented toward immediate material improvement and well-being. The same combination of a service-culture orientation and activist elitism is comfortably in place in 1875 in the program announced for the founding of Johns Hopkins University by its first president: "to prepare for the service of society a class of students who"— wherever situated—"will be wise, thoughtful, and progressive guides." It was a public fulfillment of what a dozen years earlier Henry Adams had privately called for from the world-historical perspective of his father's London embassy: "a national school of our own generation . . . to start new influences not only in politics, but in literature, in law, in society, and throughout the whole social organism of the country."

4

Not surprisingly, the most influential American philosopher for nearly a half-century after 1900, John Dewey, would make collective human betterment his guiding purpose at every stage of a long, honorable life of speculation and public advocacy; not surprisingly, popular education, democratically conceived, was the cause nearest Dewey's heart. (His major treatise, *Democracy and Education*, in 1916, was preceded in 1899 by *The School and Society*.) Dewey himself did not study in Germany. But he was at Johns Hopkins during its heroic early years, when the philosopher-genius C. S. Peirce and the experimental psychologist G. Stanley Hall taught there in company with the new-model social scientists, and when Veblen, Woodrow Wilson, and the historian Frederick Jackson Turner took advanced degrees. It was at Hopkins that Dewey began his transformation from an abstruse Hegelian idealism to the view—epitomized in his 1908 address, "Intelligence and Morals"—that philosophy's ultimate task is "to obtain more equable and comprehensive principles of action . . . in the interests of a common good." Its practitioners, Dewey insisted, are not to be content with serving merely their own discipline but must accept responsibility to the life and welfare of a society "whose conscience is its free and effectively organized intelligence." Like that other post-Hegelian, Karl Marx, Dewey meant not only to describe the world of human experience but to change it.

Of Dewey, though, it must frequently be said that his arguments as written slide somewhat too easily between analysis and prophecy and tend to state as proved or given what may only be nobly desired. In the peroration just quoted on society's "conscience," both "effectively" and "is" are promissory rather than factually descriptive. They tell us what is wanted, not what has been shown to be the case. Such use of formulated conceptions to help bring about the state of mind considered necessary to some wished-for organization of things was, of course, of the essence of American pragmatism in its popularized form (much to the annoyance of its exacting founder, Charles Sanders Peirce, who rebuked William James for terminological frivolousness and dismissed Dewey's contributions to the 1903 Chicago volume, *Studies in Logical Theory*, as so much idealized "natural history"). Pragmatism of this broader sort was as heartening a philosophy as Emersonian transcendentalism had been to an earlier American era. It could not fail to give aid and comfort to writers, artists, makers and inventors of every description, who necessarily deal in unproved assessments and imperfectly verifiable propositions. Certainly pragmatism matched and confirmed the speculative outlook of the innovative architects Louis Sullivan, whose homiletic "Kindergarten Chats" date from 1901, and Frank Lloyd Wright, whose 1941 compilation *On Architecture* restates ideas worked out forty years earlier, and equally of the Connecticut composer Charles Ives—

though all three, as in the pungent essays Ives wrote to accompany his Concord Sonata (1900–1915), tended to go directly to the Emersonian fountainhead for confirmation rather than to the newer, professionally framed arguments of Dewey and William James.

But American pragmatism, Peirce's rigorous version excepted, is also the grand modern instance of a tendency the Spanish-born Harvard philosopher George Santayana, from his invaluable outsider's perspective, attributed to the American mind in general: the tendency to entertain all its important ideas in the form of "premonitions and prophecies" and to let thought be dictated not by logical requirements but by whatever has accidentally forced itself on the thinker's personal attention. To Santayana, arguing the case in *Character and Opinion in the United States* (1920), the American intelligence displayed, all around, a settled "incapacity for education" in matters not directly touching "[its] own spontaneous life." ("United with great vitality," Santayana added, not without malice, "incapacity for education . . . is one root of idealism.") Such minds not only never arrive at a fundamental point of self-understanding but characteristically do not see that they need to; they fail to distinguish their intellectual intention from "the potency in [themselves] and in things which is about to realise that intention." As mood directs, they "oscillate between egotism and idolatry"—or, as to method, between positivism and magic—and disconcertingly identify the swervings of private willfulness, which they idealize, with reality itself. The tough-talking naturalism of the newest American thought, philosophic counterpart to the fiction of Dreiser and Jack London, was, to Santayana, merely the newest form of this premature spiritualism.

Santayana's is a telling indictment. It played its part in the flurry of national self-examination that followed the breakdown of Progressive Era confidence during and after World War I. (An endorsement of this acidulous model of the self-entrapping American will would come in the life histories chronicled after 1920 by novelists from two younger generations: Willa Cather in *A Lost Lady*, Theodore Dreiser in *An American Tragedy*, Scott Fitzgerald in *The Great Gatsby*, William Faulkner in *Absalom, Absalom!*) Santayana's own coolness toward a problem-oriented liberal humanism, with its trust in universal educability, lingers in the expressed outlook of writers as different—among those who heard him at Harvard—as Wallace Stevens and Walter Lippmann, T. S. Eliot and John Reed, none of them especially notable (as a poet like Hardy, a social analyst like the precocious Randolph Bourne are notable) for either warmth or discrimination of insight into conditional human selfhood. The cost of such studied coolness can be a troubling detachment from the actual passion and travail of mind under which, in modern society, the common life of men and women must be enacted. Given the immense new overgrowth of institutional life and the speculative constrictions of Darwinism, Marxism, anthropological or psychoanalytic determinism, to say nothing of Nietzschean inhumanism (rapidly coming into vogue toward the end of this period), what margin of freedom was left for ordinary individuality and purposefulness? On what foundation in common experience might the national commitment to an ethos of "individualism," as Tocqueville had diagnosed it, come to rest? On such questions Santayana—whose *Reason in Society* (1906) entrusts social health to a guardian-supervised change of heart among the general citizenry—had relatively little to contribute. He only (it is of course philosophy's first task) helped clear the ground, keeping speculation alert to its own unsubduable appetite for self-delusion and error.

Two whose contributions in these years to the rethinking of cultural priorities did rise from an intense and sustained personal engagement were the social-work pioneer Jane Addams and the black sociologist-historian W.E.B. Du Bois. Each, as member of a subpopulation effectively denied legal and vocational equality, was acutely sensitive to modern society's enormous power of exclusion. The radical split in the national mind that Santayana identified in "The Genteel Tradition in American Philosophy" (1911) between aggressive material enterprise and high-minded abstraction, Jane Addams perceived as, instead, a corrupting "duality of conscience." Its power "to stifle the noblest effort in the individual because his intellectual conception and his achievement are so difficult to bring together" was grounded, she wrote in *Democracy and Social Ethics* (1902), in the social order itself, above all in "the separation of the people who think from those who work." (The heroine of Louisa May Alcott's 1873 novel *Work* identifies much the same experiential gap as a major obstacle to effective reform.) Jane Addams had—as did, *a fortiori*, the sociologist Du Bois in his passionate reconstruction of the "spiritual world" of American blacks in *The Souls of Black Folk* (1903)—a richer and more immediate understanding than most philosophers of the obdurate economy of human weakness and vulnerability. She had seen first hand how men and women living too long under the threat of destitution and economic obsolescence can effectively lose their capacity for self-governing, and how young children forced into subsistence labor are deprived not simply of physical health but of their evolutionary birthright. She saw also, in educational experiments carried out at Hull House in Chicago, the residual capacity of the so-called "dangerous" classes to reassume the civil and moral powers men and women are born to. The visionary Tolstoy of *What To Do Then* touched Jane Addams's native idealism as he had touched Howells's, and led her to require of all education that it "free the powers of each man and connect him with the rest of life." A truly popular education would thus perform the comprehensive function Du Bois eloquently claimed for the Negro churches (*The Souls of Black Folk*, chapter 10), giving both personal and collective expression to the ethical life and aspiration of a whole people.

By comparison, the more conventionally articulated social and behavioral thought of the liberal publicist Herbert Croly—whose manifesto, *The Promise of American Life* (1909), projected a transformation of the Progressivist reform impulse into a systematized politics of national reconstruction—and even of the humanely eloquent Josiah Royce in philosophy, is likely to seem synthetic and, in application, more wishful than realistically observant. (Nobly wishful in Royce's case; humankind would indeed be better off if by acts of will it could march down the path outlined in Royce's 1901 *summa*, *The World and the Individual*, toward a fulfillment at once individual and social.) Croly, who inherited notions of a rationally engineered human solidarity from his father's dedication to Auguste Comte's mid-nineteenth-century religion of humanity, feared one consequence in particular of the modern industrial division of labor and the drive toward corporate concentration; this was the massive subdividing of the civil population into specialized functions and subgroups without capacity of their own to negotiate "a wholesome national balance." He thus identified a modern socioeconomic dilemma for which, soon after, fascism would emerge in Europe as the unacceptable political solution. In contrast, Croly's own proposals for technological and managerial efficiency were designed to make democracy work, not to replace it.

To what degree democracy remained workable under the aggrandizements of modern industrial capitalism is a question that seems less important in the writings of Thorstein Veblen (though Veblen does ask it) than does a cultural anthropologist's quizzical curiosity about the process itself of institutional adaptation and change. Allied to the rhetorical irony that concentrated his readers' attention on such gestural phenomena of modern life as "conspicuous consumption" or—defining industrial sabotage—"the conscientious withdrawal of efficiency," Veblen's neo-Darwinian analyses of the behavior of business society's leisure class (1899) and of American business enterprise as an ideological system (1904) quickly became part of the new century's enduring folklore. His moralized distinction between *engineer*, hero of disinterested creativity, and *financier*, manipulative and parasitic, has the imaginative authority of great fiction, and his celebration of the human species' indestructible "instinct of workmanship" mythopoeically balances the world-historical pessimism of his 1914 treatise bearing that title. Small wonder that as much as any other figure Veblen became the moral hero of the dispiriting panorama of John Dos Passos's 1930s trilogy, *U.S.A.*

Something of the same difference in force and penetration of understanding can strike us in comparing the philosophic legacy of Royce and of his older Cambridge (but not Harvard) contemporary, Charles Sanders Peirce. Much of Peirce's writing was too rigorously specialized to claim general attention—though his important early essays, "The Fixation of Belief" and "How to Make Our Ideas Clear," appeared in 1877–78 in *Popular Science Monthly*, the journal of the American Spencerians. (The mass of Peirce's difficult thought, once regarded as eccentric, is under admiring reexamination in our own semiology-fixated era.) Writing discursively, Peirce considered it a matter of methodological probity to argue by means of opaque neologisms whose sheer ugliness would repel anyone grubbing about for philosophic shortcuts. When his friend William James transformed "pragmatism" from a rule in logic into an all-purpose intellectual attitude, Peirce at once renamed his own concept "pragmaticism" and reproved James for being insufficiently attentive to "the moral aspect of terminology."

On the great emergent issue of existential trust, which in one form or another still dominates the unresolved ideological and spiritual debates of our headlong century—the issue, that is, of whether the active human consciousness can find its own footing and organize a liveable destiny within the depersonalizing expansions of modern globalized history—Royce, who gratefully borrowed Peirce's mathematics in postulating how individual selves might hold position within an infinitely expanding totality, fell back for psychological and ethical support on a "philosophy of loyalty" (1908). Loyalty—to some truth or truths, to the human collectivity, to existence itself—is affirmed as a vital and sufficient *principle* of behavior chiefly because, unlike the ethical "inner check" coincidentally propounded at Harvard by the self-proclaimed new humanist Irving Babbitt, it is so evidently a primal human *need* and *appetite*. All Royce's considerable forensic skill goes to establishing loyalty as the best, because most natural, solution to both spiritual and societal alienation, though contradictorily one whole chapter is devoted to the necessity of organizing extended training in such loyalty, in the surrender of selfhood to causes outside itself. (Another who in these years fixed attention on the problem—in a postreligious age—of reattaching human selfhood to some greater existential whole was the University of Michigan social psychologist Charles Horton Cooley, whose widely popular book on the socialization of personality, *Human Nature and the Social Order* [1902], explores the double premise, or truism, that "a separate individual is an abstraction unknown to experience, and so likewise is society when regarded as something apart from individuals.")

But Peirce had realized from the beginning that an ethical truth and discipline needing so much explanatory inculcation would not in and of itself stave off behavioral confusion and doubt. Peirce's starting point was the recognizably Emersonian, and Kantian, principle that what in our sentient and intellective life we are obliged to do, we are—so far as may be known—already constituted to do. By formidable reasoning his 1903 lectures on pragmatism arrive at his own version of Emerson's intellectual *point d'appui* in the crucial sixth chapter of *Nature* (1836), which was simply that "God never jests with us." Everywhere in existence, Peirce declares, we will find "an element of Reasonableness to which we can train our own reason to conform more and more . . .":

> . . . we need not wait until it is proved that there is a reason operative in experience to which our own can approximate. We should at once hope that it is so, since in that hope lies the only possibility of any knowledge.

For Peirce as for Emerson, such "hope," which in the vernacular seems frail and unstable—"the thing with feathers," Emily Dickinson's verse-meditation on it begins—is nevertheless the very engine of active, creative being.

So was it also for William James, the man "born afresh every morning" (his redoubtable sister Alice's double-edged appraisal). It is fitting that an account of American intellectual life during the half-century after the Civil War should end with James, who became as ebulliently persuasive a writer of speculative prose as our society has produced, a fluent master of both technical and popular exposition. James's insistence on submitting every reflective issue to the test of common and immediate experience was already established when in 1880, precisely as regards hope and its painful contraries, he announced to the Harvard Philosophical Club that "the permanent presence of the sense of futurity in the mind has been strangely ignored by most [philosophic] writers" ("The Sentiment of Rationality"). "The fact is," he continued, "that our consciousness at a given moment is never free from the ingredient of expectancy." How consciousness actually behaves at given moments was William James's lifelong preoccupation. It regulates both of his masterworks, *Principles of Psychology* (1890), with its brilliantly specific evocations of ordinary mental behavior, and *The Varieties of Religious Experience* (1902), the abounding openmindedness of which rises from an intensely personal sense of the "inner authority and illumination" characterizing spiritual transactions however disorienting they may seem, however disconnected from the rest of life. James was so respectful of immediately experienceable reality that in a later essay, "Does 'Consciousness' Exist?" which Alfred North Whitehead saw as completing the long revolution out of Cartesian positivism, he could deliver an unabashed *no* to the question whether consciousness-as-such could be treated by speculative thinkers as any sort of substantial or unitary entity.

The power to make robust negations, even at one's own vital expense— to say *no* in blood as well as in thunder—was for William James a test of intellectual maturity and a prerequisite to any truly productive thinking. "It seems almost as if it were necessary to become worthless as a practical being," he wrote in "On a Certain Blindness in Human Beings" (1899), "if one is to hope to attain any breadth of insight into the impersonal world of worths as such." No more than in his brother Henry's fictional narratives of the "finer grain" of consciousness and moral feeling are social and historical concerns likely to be what is most directly at issue in William James's writing. Where the focus of concern is on institutional oppression and subornation, James's pragmatic ethic cannot finally escape a suspicion that it may be an ethic for those already privileged with a relative freedom. Yet he understood very well how it is in the interest of institutional and collective health as well as of private satisfaction that "the energies of men" (the title of his presidential address to the American Philosophical Association in 1906) find full and natural release. So in a characteristically provocative address at the end of his life he defined the whole issue of human survival in the new era of global imperialism as one of developing not a mass instinct for "pacificism"—something that seemed to him against the grain of the fallible human spirit—but a "moral equivalent of war" (1910). (*Ad bellum purificandum*: thus would his truest American inheritor, Kenneth Burke, inscribe his own monumental study of the varieties of human expressiveness and expressive coexistence.)

Extraordinarily different in temper and style from either Peirce's argumentative severity or Veblen's implacable moral naturalism, William James's thinking wonderfully complements theirs in its open-minded candor. Its workaday indifference to its own imperfections still offers a bracing model for (so to speak) staying the course, individually or collectively, against any odds. And in its unflagging grace of style it articulates all the more directly the supple intellectual courage that within their American generation broke essential ground for the renaissance in imaginative literature of 1912 and after—for the confident, self-planted originality of, at their best, Stein, Lewis, Cather, Hemingway, Fitzgerald, and Faulkner in prose fiction; and of Eliot, Stevens, Frost, Pound, Hart Crane, and Marianne Moore in the practice and understanding of poetry.

Permissions

Index